£2

29/12

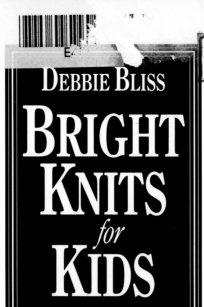

DEBBIE BLISS

BRIGHT KNITS
for
KIDS

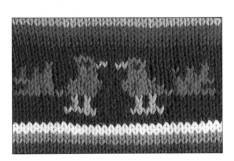

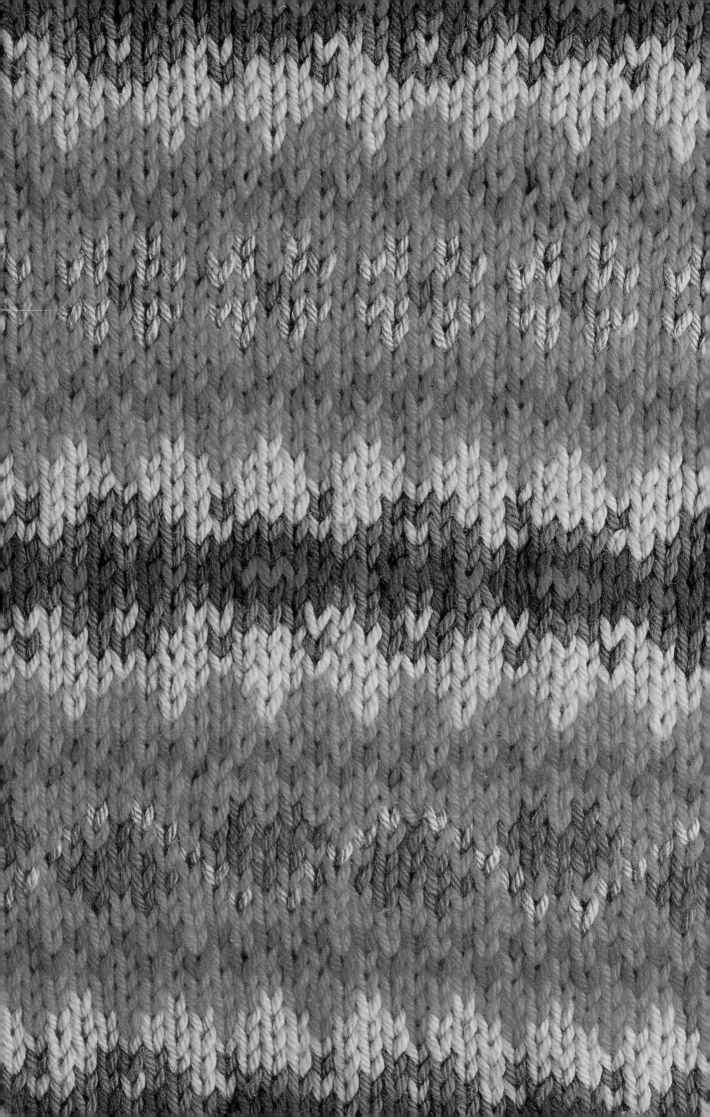

Debbie Bliss

Bright Knits for Kids

COLLINS & BROWN

For William, Eleanor and Pat

First published in Great Britain in 1996 by
Collins & Brown Limited,
London House, Great Eastern Wharf,
Parkgate Road, London SW11 4NQ

Photography and illustrations © Collins & Brown Limited 1996
Editor: Jane Struthers
Art Director: Carole Perks
Photographer: Sandra Lousada
Stylist: Marie Willey
Illustrators: Stephen Dew and Pentrix Design
Pattern Checker: Tina Egleton

British Library Cataloguing in Publication Data:
A catalogue record for this book is available from the British Library

ISBN 1 85470 245 9 (paperback edition)
ISBN 1 85585 275 6 (hardback edition)

Typeset in Great Britain by Bookworm Typesetting, Manchester
Colour reproduction by Master Image, Singapore
Printed and bound in Spain

Contents

Introduction

This book is a celebration of colour. There are over 25 designs ranging from cotton Fair Isles in hot, spicy brights to vivid tartan, subtly shaded ginghams and folkloric florals.

There are beautiful ranges of yarn available to knitters now, and colour can transform even the classics – the much-loved Aran looks fresh and new in turquoise or lime and a Guernsey takes on new life in glowing red. Children look wonderful in primary colours but there is a broader palette to choose from too, from

usky terracottas and golds to faded blues nd soft greens.

For the knitter who prefers stitch detail o colour patterning there are textured and abled designs, and for those who are nsure of their Fair Isle or Jacquard echniques there are simple stripes.

The designs cover an age range from abies to six-year-olds but I have given enerous allowance on the sizings as I believe that children should feel comfortable and unrestricted when wearing handknits. As all the patterns quote actual measurements, knitters can choose to make whichever size they prefer.

Debbie Bliss

THE KIDS

Jacket with
Moss Stitch Yoke
10   see page 45

Seaside Sweater
see page 46   11

Spicy Fair Isle Sweater
12   see page 48

Cabled Rib Sweater
see page 49   13

Vertical Stripe Sweater

14 see page 50

Floral and
Fair Isle Cardigan
see page 51   15

Sampler Cardigan
16   see page 52

Rugby Shirt
see page 54 17

Shawl-collared
Fair Isle Jacket
20   see page 55

Aran Coat
see page 56

Bird Jacket and Hat
22   see page 58

Rose Jacket
see page 59   23

Guernsey-style
Sweater
24   see page 61

Fair Isle Waistcoat
see page 62   25

Striped Top with
Sailor Collar
26   see page 63

Zipped Fair Isle
Jacket with Hat
see page 64   27

Gingham Jacket
30   see page 66

Cable and Bobble
Aran Sweater

 see page 68

Patterned Coat
see page 69   33

Star Sweater
34   see page 70

Aran Cardigan with
Tie Collar
see page 72   35

Tartan All-in-one
with Beret
36   see page 74

Bright Fair Isle Cardigan
with Beret
see page 75   37

Sandals
see page 77 39

Tulip Jacket
40   see page 77

Brilliant White Shirt
see page 78   41

THE KNITS

Basic Information

NOTES

Figures for larger sizes are given in () brackets. Where only one figure appears, this applies to all sizes.

Work figures given in [] brackets the number of times stated afterwards. Alternatively, they give the resultant number of stitches.

Where 0 appears, no stitches or rows are worked for this size.

The yarn amounts given in the instructions are based on average requirements and should therefore be considered approximate. If you want to use a substitute yarn, choose a yarn of the same type and weight as the one recommended. The following descriptions of the various Rowan yarns are meant as a guide to the yarn weight and type (i.e. cotton, mohair, wool, etc.). Remember that the description of the yarn weight is only a rough guide and you should always test a yarn first to see if it will achieve the correct tension (gauge).

Magpie Aran: a fisherman medium-weight yarn (100% pure new wool) approx. 150m/164yd per 100g/3¾oz hank.

Cotton Glace: a lightweight cotton yarn (100% cotton) approx. 112m/123yd per 50g/1¾oz ball.

Designer DK: a double knitting weight yarn (100% pure new wool) approx. 115m/125yd per 50g/1¾oz ball.

Handknit DK Cotton: a medium-weight cotton yarn (100% cotton) approx. 85m/90yd per 50g/1¾oz ball.

Lightweight DK: a lightweight double knitting weight yarn (100% pure new wool) approx. 67.5m/75yd per 25g/1oz hank.

The amount of a substitute yarn needed is determined by the number of metres/yards required rather than by the number of grams/ounces. If you are unsure when choosing a suitable substitute, ask your yarn shop to advise you.

TENSION

Each pattern in this book specifies tension – the number of stitches and rows per centimetre/inch that should be obtained on the given needles, yarn and stitch pattern. Check your tension carefully before commencing work.

Use the same yarn, needles and stitch pattern as those to be used for main work and knit a sample at least 12.5 x 12.5 cm/5in square. Smooth out the finished sample on a flat surface but do not stretch it. To check the tension, place a ruler horizontally on the sample and mark 10cm/4in across with pins. Count the number of stitches between the pins. To check the row tension, place the ruler vertically on the sample and mark out 10cm/4in with pins. Count the number of rows between the pins. If the number of stitches and rows is greater than specified, try again using larger needles; if less, use smaller needles.

The stitch tension is the most important element to get right.

The following terms may be unfamiliar to US readers:

UK terms	US terms
Aran wool	*"fisherman" (unbleached wool) yarn*
ball band	*yarn wrapper*
cast off	*bind off*
DK wool	*knitting worsted yarn*
double crochet stitch	*single crochet stitch*
make up (garment)	*finish (garment)*
rib	*ribbing*
stocking stitch	*stockinette stitch*
tension	*gauge*
waistcoat	*vest*

In the US balls or hanks of yarn are sold in ounces, not in grams; the weights of the relevant Rowan Yarns are given on this page.

In addition, a few specific knitting and crochet terms may be unfamiliar to some readers. The list on this page explains the abbreviations used in this book to help the reader understand how to follow the various stitches and stages.

STANDARD ABBREVIATIONS

alt = alternate; **beg** = begin(ning); **cont** = continue; **dec** = decreas(e)ing; **foll** = following; **inc** = increas(e)ing; **k** = knit; **m1** = make one by picking up loop lying between st just worked and next st and work into the back of it; **patt** = pattern; = purl; **psso** = pass slipped st over; **rem** = remain(ing); **rep** = repeat; **skpo** = slip one, k1, pass slipped st over; **sl** = slip; **st(s)** = stitch(es); **st st** = stocking stitch; **tbl** = through back of loop(s); **tog** = together; **yb** = yarn back; **yf** = yarn forward; **yon** = yarn over needle; **yrn** = yarn round needle

IMPORTANT

Check on ball band for washing instructions. After washing, pat garment into shape and dry flat away from direct heat.

ATERIALS

(10) x 50g balls of Rowan DK
andknit Cotton.
pair each of 3¼mm (No 10/US 3) and
nm (No 8/US 6) knitting needles.
rochet hook.
buttons.

EASUREMENTS

fit age	3–4	5–6	years
ctual chest	83	89	cm
easurement	32¾	35	in
ength	36	41	cm
	14¼	16¼	in
eeve seam	30	34	cm
	12	13½	in

ENSION

sts and 28 rows to 10cm/4in square
er st st on 4mm (No 8/US 6) needles.

BBREVIATIONS

e page 44.

BACK

With 3¼mm (No 10/US 3) needles, cast on
73 (79) sts.
1st row: K1, [p1, k1] to end.
This row forms moss st patt. Rep this row
11 times more, inc 2 sts evenly across last
row. [75 (81) sts.]
Change to 4mm (No 8/US 6) needles.
Beg with a k row, work in st st, inc 1 st at
each end of 3rd row and every foll 4th row
until there are 83 (89) sts. Cont straight
until Back measures 18 (22)cm/7¼ (8¾)in
from beg, ending with a p row.
Shape Armholes
Cast off 4 sts at beg of next 2 rows. [75
(81) sts.] Cont straight until Back measures
25 (29)cm/10 (11½)in from beg, ending
with a p row.
Now work in moss st patt until Back
measures 36 (41)cm/14¼ (16¼)in from
beg, ending with a wrong side row.
Shape Shoulders
Cast off 13 (14) sts at beg of next 2 rows
and 12 (13) sts at beg of foll 2 rows. Leave
rem 25 (27) sts on a holder.

LEFT FRONT

With 3¼mm (No 10/US 3) needles, cast on
37 (41) sts. Work 12 rows in moss st patt
as given for Back welt, inc 2 sts evenly
across last row. [39 (43) sts.]
Change to 4mm (No 8/US 6) needles.
Next row: K to last 6 sts, moss st 6.
Next row: Moss st 6, p to end.
These 2 rows form patt. Cont in patt, inc 1
st at side edge on next row and every foll
4th row until there are 43 (47) sts. Cont
straight until Front matches Back to
armhole shaping, ending at side edge.
Shape Armhole
Cast off 4 sts at beg of next row. [39 (43)
sts.] Cont straight until Front measures 25
(29)cm/10 (11½)in from beg, ending with a
wrong side row.
Now work in moss st patt across all sts until
Front measures 29 (34)cm/11½ (13½)in
from beg, ending at armhole edge.
Shape Neck
Next row: Patt to last 6 sts, turn; slip the 6
sts on to a safety pin.
Dec 1 st at neck edge on next 5 rows then

on every alt row until 25 (27) sts rem. Cont
straight until Front matches Back to
shoulder shaping, ending at armhole edge.
Shape Shoulder
Cast off 13 (14) sts at beg of next row.
Work 1 row. Cast off rem 12 (13) sts.
Mark front band to indicate position of 5
buttons: first one 6 rows up from lower
edge, last one 1cm/¼in below neck shaping
and rem 3 evenly spaced between.

RIGHT FRONT

With 3¼mm (No 10/US 3) needles, cast on
37 (41) sts. Work 6 rows in moss st patt as
given for Back welt.
Buttonhole row (right side): Patt 2, k2
tog, yf, patt to end.
Work a further 5 rows in moss st patt, inc 2
sts evenly across last row. [39 (43) sts.]
Change to 4mm (No 8/US 6) needles.
Next row: Moss st 6, k to end.
Next row: P to last 6 sts, moss st 6.
Complete as given for Left Front, working
buttonholes at markers as before.

SLEEVES

With 3¼mm (No 10/US 3) needles, cast on
35 (39) sts. Work 11 rows in moss st patt
as given for Back welt.
Inc row: Moss st 3 (5), [m1, k4] to last 4
(6) sts, m1, moss st 4 (6). [43 (47) sts.]
Change to 4mm (No 8/US 6) needles.
Beg with a k row, work in st st, inc 1 st at
each end of 3rd row and every foll 4th row
until there are 75 (79) sts. Cont straight
until Sleeve measures 30 (34)cm/12
(13½)in from beg, ending with a p row.
Cast off.

COLLAR

Join shoulder seams.
With right side facing and using 4mm (No
8/US 6) needles, slip 6 sts from Right Front
safety pin on to needle, pick up and k21
(24) sts up right front neck, work across
back neck sts as follows: [k2, k twice in
next st] 8 times, k1 (3), pick up and k21
(24) sts down left front neck, then moss st
across sts on Left Front safety pin. [87 (95)
sts.]
Next row: Moss st 8, k 71 (79), moss st 8.
Next row: Cast off 4, moss st 3 sts more,
p57 (62), turn.
Next row: K43 (45), turn.
Next row: P46 (48), turn.
Next row: K49 (51), turn.
Cont in this way, working 3 sts more at end
of next 6 (8) rows, turn, p to last 8 sts,
moss st 8.
Next row: Cast off 4, moss st 3 sts more, k
to last 4 sts, moss st 4. [79 (87) sts.]
Next row: Moss st 4, p to last 4 sts, moss
st 4.
Next row: Moss st 4, m1, k to last 4 sts,
m1, moss st 4.
Next row: Moss st 4, p to last 4 sts, moss
st 4.
Next row: Moss st 4, k to last 4 sts, moss
st 4.
Rep last 4 rows twice more. Now work 5
rows in moss st across all sts. Cast off
loosely in patt.

acket with Moss Stitch Yoke

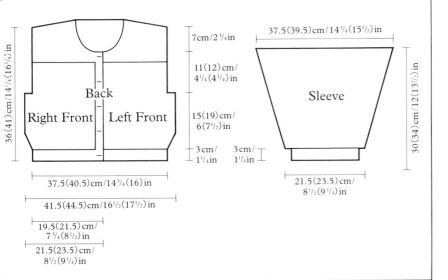

POCKETS (make 2)

With 4mm (No 8/US 6) needles, cast on 23 sts. Work 9cm/3½in in moss st as given for Back welt. Cast off.
With right side facing and using crochet hook, work 1 row of double crochet around 3 sides of pocket, omitting cast off edge. Do not turn. Work 1 row of backward double crochet (double crochet worked from left to right). Fasten off.

POCKET FLAPS (make 2)

With 4mm (No 8/US 6) needles, cast on 23 sts. Work 4cm/1½in in moss st as given for Back welt. Dec 1 st at each end of next 6 rows.
Buttonhole row: Work 2 tog, patt 3, yf, k2 tog, patt 2, work 2 tog.
Dec 1 st at each end of next 3 rows. Work 3 tog and fasten off.
Omitting cast on edge, work crochet edging around flaps as given for Pockets.

WELT STRAPS (make 2)

With 4mm (No 8/US 6) needles, cast on 7 sts. Work 8cm/3in in moss st as given for Back welt.
Buttonhole row: Patt 3, yf, k2 tog, patt 2. Patt 2 rows. Dec 1 st at each end of next 2 rows. Work 3 tog and fasten off.
Omitting cast on edge, work crochet edging around straps as given for Pockets.

TO MAKE UP

Sew in sleeves, placing centre of sleeves to shoulder seams and sewing last 6 row ends of sleeve tops to cast off sts at armholes. Place straps on top of front welts and sew cast on edges to side of welts. Join side and sleeve seams. Sew on pockets and pocket flaps. Sew on buttons to front band, each pocket and front welt straps.

Seaside Sweater page 11

MATERIALS

8 (9) x 50g balls of Rowan DK Handknit Cotton in Navy (A).
2 (3) balls in White (B).
1 pair each of 3¼mm (No 10/US 3), 3¾mm (No 9/US 5) and 4mm (No 8/US 6) knitting needles.

MEASUREMENTS

To fit age	2–3	4–5	years
Actual chest	81	91	cm
measurement	32	36	in
Length	37	42	cm
	14½	16½	in
Sleeve seam	22	26	cm
	8¾	10¼	in

TENSION

20 sts and 28 rows to 10cm/4in square over st st on 4mm (No 8/US 6) needles.

ABBREVIATIONS

mb = make bobble as follows: [k1, p1, k1, p1] all in next st, then pass 2nd, 3rd and 4th st over first st.
Also see page 44.

NOTE

Read charts from right to left on right side (k) rows and from left to right on wrong side (p) rows. When working in two-colour rib and border pattern, strand yarn not in use loosely across wrong side over no more than 5 sts to keep fabric elastic. Use separate length of B yarn for each motif when working in main pattern and twist yarns together on wrong side at joins to avoid holes.

BACK

With 3¼mm (No 10/US 3) needles and A, cast on 78 (86) sts.
Work in two-colour rib as follows:
1st row (right side): P2A, [k2B, p2A] to end.
2nd row: K2A, [p2B, k2A] to end.

Rep last 2 rows 4 times more, inc 3 (5) sts evenly across last row. [81 (91) sts.]
Change to 4mm (No 8/US 6) needles.
Work border patt as follows:
1st row: K in A.
2nd row: P in A.
3rd row: K5A, [1B, 9A] to last 6 sts, 1B, 5A.
4th row: P4A, [1B, 1A, 1B, 7A] to last 7 sts, 1B, 1A, 1B, 4A.
5th row: With A, mb, k2A, [1B, 3A, 1B, 2A, with A, mb, 2A] to last 8 sts, [1B, 3A] twice.
6th row: P2A, [1B, 5A, 1B, 3A] to last 9 sts, 1B, 5A, 1B, 2A.
7th row: K1A, [1B, 3A, with A, mb, 3A, 1B, 1A] to end.
8th row: P1B, [9A, 1B] to end.
Work in main patt as follows:
Beg with a k row, work 2 (6) rows in st st and A.
Next row: K42 (47)A, k across 1st row of chart 1, k12 (17)A.
Next row: P12 (17)A, p across 2nd row of chart 1, p42 (47)A.
Work a further 13 rows as set.
Next row: P12 (17)A, p across 16th row of chart 1, p6 (11) A, p across 1st row of chart 2, p13A.
Next row: K13A, k across 2nd row of chart 2, k6 (11)A, k across 17th row of chart 1, k12 (17)A.
Work a further 5 rows as set.

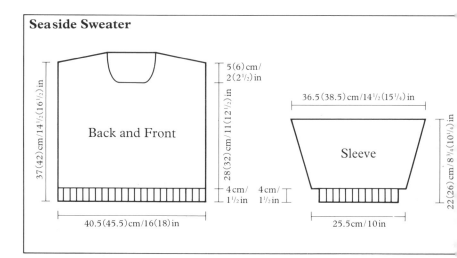

Seaside Sweater

Back and Front
37 (42) cm/14½ (16½) in
28 (32) cm/11 (12½) in
5 (6) cm/ 2 (2½) in
4 cm/ 1½ in
40.5 (45.5) cm/16 (18) in

Sleeve
36.5 (38.5) cm/14½ (15¼) in
22 (26) cm/8¾ (10¼) in
4 cm/ 1½ in
25.5 cm/10 in

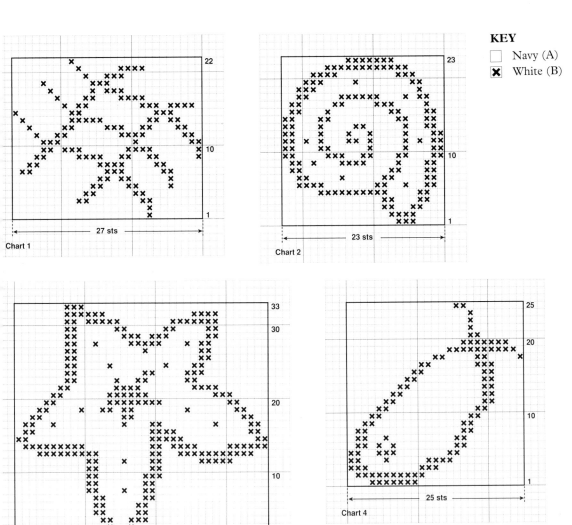

KEY

☐ Navy (A)

☒ White (B)

Chart 1 — 27 sts

Chart 2 — 23 sts

Chart 3 — 36 sts

Chart 4 — 25 sts

ext row: K13A, k across 8th row of chart
k45 (55)A.

ext row: P45 (55)A, p across 9th row of
art 2, p13A.

ork a further 4 (8) rows as set.

ext row: K13A, k across 14th (18th) row of
chart 2, k0 (10)A, k across 1st row of
art 3, k9A.

ext row: P9A, p across 2nd row of chart
p0 (10)A, p across 15th (19th) row of
art 2, p13A.

ork a further 8 (4) rows as set.

ext row: K36 (46)A, k across 11th (7th)
w of chart 3, k9A.

ext row: P9A, p across 12th (8th) row of
art 3, p36 (46)A.

ork a further 14 (20) rows as set.

ext row: K8A, k across 1st row of chart
k3 (13)A, k across 27th (29th) row of
art 3, k9A.

ext row: P9A, p across 28th (30th) row of
chart 3, p3 (13)A, p across 2nd row of
art 4, p8A.

ork a further 5 (3) rows as set.

ext row: P48 (58)A, p across 8th (6th)
w of chart 4, p8A.

ext row: K8A, k across 9th (7th) row of
art 4, k48 (58)A. **

ork a further 16 (18) rows as set.

ont in A only, work 3 (7) rows.

hape Shoulders

ast off 13 (15) sts at beg of next 4 rows.

ave rem 29 (31) sts on a holder.

RONT

ork as given for Back to **. Work a

further 5 (7) rows as set.

Shape Neck

Next row: Patt 33 (37), turn.
Work on this set of sts only. Dec 1 st at
neck edge on next 4 rows then on 3 foll alt
rows. [26 (30) sts.] Cont in A only, work 3
(7) rows straight.

Shape Shoulder

Cast off 13 (15) sts at beg of next row.
Work 1 row. Cast off rem 13 (15) sts.
With right side facing, slip centre 15 (17)
sts on to a holder, rejoin yarn to rem sts
and patt to end. Dec 1 st at neck edge on
next 4 rows, then on 3 foll alt rows. [26
(30) sts.] Cont in A only, work 4 (7) rows
straight. Complete as given for first side.

SLEEVES

With 3¼mm (No 10/US 3) needles and A,
cast on 42 (46) sts. Work 10 rows in two-
colour rib as given for Back welt.
Change to 4mm (No 8/US 6) needles.

Inc row: K5, m1, [k4 (9), m1] to last 5 sts,
k5. [51 sts.]

Beg with a 2nd row, work border patt as
given for Back, inc 1 st at each end of 4th
row. [53 sts.]

Work in main patt as follows:

Beg with a k row, work 2 (6) rows in st st
and A, inc 1 st at each end of 1st row and
foll 4th row on **2nd size** only. [55 (57) sts.]

Next row: K28 (29)A, k across 1st row of
chart 1, k0 (1)A.

Next row: P0 (1)A, p across 2nd row of
chart 1, p28 (29)A.

Work a further 15 rows as set, inc 1 st at

each end of next row and 3 foll 4th rows,
working inc sts in A. [63 (65) sts.]

Next row: P4 (5)A, p across 18th row of
chart 1, p2A, p across 1st row of chart 2, p7
(8)A.

Next row: With A, inc in 1st st, k6 (7)A, k
across 2nd row of chart 2, k2A, k across
19th row of chart 1, with A, k3 (4), inc in
last st. [65 (67) sts.]

Work a further 3 rows as set.

Next row: With A, inc in 1st st, k7 (8)A, k
across 6th row of chart 2, with A, k33 (34),
inc in last st.

Next row: P35 (36)A, p across 7th row of
chart 2, p9 (10)A.

Work a further 16 rows as set, inc 1 st at
each end of 3rd row and 2 (3) foll 4th rows.
[73 (77) sts.] Cont in A only, work 2 (8)
rows. Cast off.

NECKBAND

Join right shoulder seam.
With right side facing, using 3¾mm (No
9/US 5) needles and A, pick up and k19
(21) sts down left front neck, k centre front
sts, pick up and k19 (21) sts up right front
neck, k back neck sts. [82 (90) sts.]
P 1 row. Beg with a 1st row, work 6 rows in
two-colour rib as given for Back welt. With
A, cast off in rib.

TO MAKE UP

Join left shoulder and neckband seam. Sew
on sleeves, placing centre of sleeves to
shoulder seams. Join side and sleeve seams.

47

Spicy Fair Isle Sweater page 12

MATERIALS
5 (6) x 50g balls of Rowan DK Handknit Cotton in Orange (A).
3 (4) balls in Gold (B).
2 balls in Dark Pink.
1 ball each in Lime, Pale Blue, Dark Green and Dark Blue.
1 pair each of 3¼mm (No 10/US 3) and 4mm (No 8/US 6) knitting needles.

MEASUREMENTS

To fit age	4–6	6–8	years
Actual chest measurement	90 35½	95 37½	cm in
Length	42 16½	47 18½	cm in
Sleeve seam	31 12¼	34 13½	cm in

TENSION
22 sts and 25 rows to 10cm/4in square over pattern on 4mm (No 8/US 6) needles.

ABBREVIATIONS
See page 44.

NOTE
Read chart from right to left on right side (k) rows and from left to right on wrong side (p) rows. When working in pattern, strand the yarn not in use loosely across wrong side over no more than 5 sts to keep fabric elastic.

BACK
With 3¼mm (No 10/US 3) needles and A, cast on 98 (102) sts. Beg with a k row, work 4 rows in st st. Change to B.
1st row (right side): K2, [p2, k2] to end.
2nd row: P2, [k2, p2] to end.
Rep last 2 rows twice more, inc 1 (3) sts

evenly across last row. [99 (105) sts.]
Change to 4mm (No 8/US 6) needles. Beg with a k row, work in st st and patt from chart until Back measures 42 (47)cm/16½ (18½)in from beg, ending with a wrong side row.
Shape Shoulders
Cast off 16 (17) sts at beg of next 4 rows. Leave rem 35 (37) sts on a holder.

FRONT
Work as given for Back until Front measures 36 (40)cm/14¼ (15¾)in from beg, ending with a wrong side row.
Shape Neck
Next row: Patt 40 (42), turn.
Work on this set of sts only. Dec 1 st at neck edge on next 6 rows then on 2 foll alt rows. [32 (34) sts.] Cont straight until Front matches Back to shoulder shaping, ending at side edge.
Shape Shoulder
Cast off 16 (17) sts at beg of next row. Work 1 row. Cast off rem 16 (17) sts. With right side facing, slip centre 19 (21) sts on to a holder, rejoin yarn to rem sts and patt to end. Complete as first side.

SLEEVES
With 3¼mm (No 10/US 3) needles and A, cast on 46 (50) sts. Beg with a k row, work 4 rows in st st. Change to B and work 10 rows in rib as given for Back, inc 3 sts evenly across last row. [49 (53) sts.]

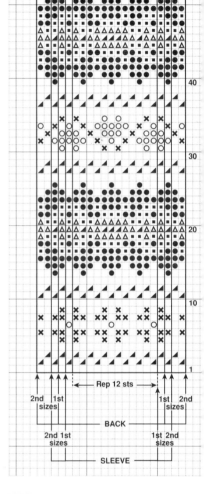

KEY

☐	Orange (A)	⊙	Pale Blue
●	Gold (B)	▪	Dark Green
◤	Dark Pink	△	Dark Blue
✕	Lime		

Change to 4mm (No 8/US 6) needles. Beg with a k row, work in st st and patt from chart, inc 1 st at each end of 5th row and every foll 4th row until there are 73 (79) sts, working inc sts into patt. Cont straight until Sleeve measures 31 (34)cm/12¼ (13½)in from beg, ending with a wrong side row. Cast off.

NECKBAND
Join right shoulder seam.
With right side facing, using 3¼mm (No 10/US 3) needles and B, pick up and k16 (18) sts down left front neck, k centre front sts, pick up and k16 (18) sts up right front neck, then k back neck sts. [86 (94) sts.] Beg with a 2nd row, work 7 rows in rib as given for Back. Change to A. Beg with a k row, work 4 rows in st st. Cast off loosely.

TO MAKE UP
Join left shoulder and neckband seam, reversing seam on st st section of neckband. Sew in sleeves, placing centre of sleeves to shoulder seams. Join side and sleeve seam, reversing seams on st st section of welt and cuffs.

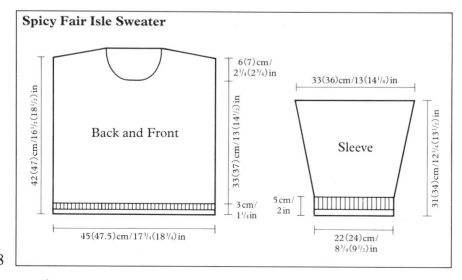

Spicy Fair Isle Sweater

Back and Front
42(47)cm/16½(18½)in
45(47.5)cm/17¾(18¾)in
3cm/1¼in

Sleeve
6(7)cm/2¼(2¾)in
33(36)cm/13(14¼)in
33(37)cm/13(14½)in
31(34)cm/12¼(13½)in
5cm/2in
22(24)cm/8¾(9½)in

;abled Rib Sweater page 13

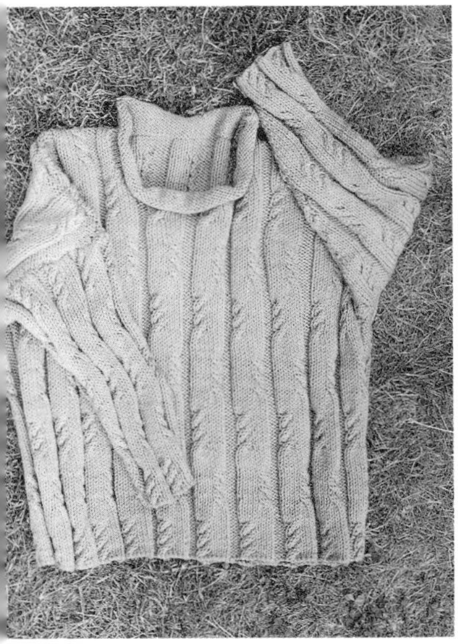

ATERIALS

(12) x 50g balls of Rowan DK
.ndknit Cotton.
›air each of 3¼mm (No 10/US 3) and
ım (No 8/US 6) knitting needles.
ble needle.

EASUREMENTS

› fit age	3–4	5–6	years
tual chest ›asurement	88 34¾	97 38	cm in
ngth	39 15¼	43 17	cm in
:eve seam	22 8¾	27 10¾	cm in

:NSION

sts and 28 rows to 10cm/4in square
er pattern on 4mm (No 8/US 6)
edles.

3BREVIATIONS

4B = slip next 2 sts on to cable needle
d leave at back of work, k2, then k2
›m cable needle;
4F = slip next 2 sts on to cable needle
d leave at front of work, k2, then k2
›m cable needle.
so see page 44.

BACK

With 4mm (No 8/US 6) needles, cast on 114 (126) sts.
1st row (right side): P5, [k8, p4] to last st, p1.
2nd row: K5, [p8, k4] to last st, k1.
3rd row: P5, [k4, C4B, p4] to last st, p1.
4th row: As 2nd row.
5th to 12th rows: Rep 1st to 4th rows twice.
13th to 18th rows: Rep 1st and 2nd rows 3 times.
19th row: P5, [C4F, k4, p4] to last st, p1.
20th row: As 2nd row.
21st and 22nd rows: As 1st and 2nd rows.
23rd to 30th rows: Rep 19th to 22nd rows twice.
31st and 32nd rows: As 1st and 2nd rows.
These 32 rows form patt. Cont in patt until Back measures 39 (43)cm/15¼ (17)in from beg, ending with a wrong side row.
Shape Shoulders
Cast off 20 (22) sts at beg of next 2 rows and 21 (23) sts at beg of foll 2 rows. Leave rem 32 (36) sts on a holder.

FRONT

Work as given for Back until Front measures 34 (36)cm/13¼ (14¼)in from beg, ending with a wrong side row.
Shape Neck
Next row: Patt 48 (52), turn.
Work on this set of sts only. Keeping patt correct, dec 1 st at neck edge on every row until 41 (45) sts rem. Cont straight until Front matches Back to shoulder shaping, ending at side edge.
Shape Shoulder
Cast off 20 (22) sts at beg of next row.
Work 1 row. Cast off rem 21 (23) sts.
With right side facing, slip centre 18 (22) sts on to a holder, rejoin yarn to rem sts, patt to end. Complete as given for first side.

SLEEVES

With 4mm (No 8/US 6) needles, cast on 46 (52) sts.
1st row (right side): P1 (4), [k8, p4] to last 9 (12) sts, k8, p1 (4).
2nd row: K1 (4), [p8, k4] to last 9 (12) sts, p8, k1 (4).
These 2 rows set position of patt. Cont in patt, inc 1 st at each end of next row and every foll 2nd row until there are 76 (72) sts, then on every foll 3rd row until there are 90 (100) sts, working inc sts into patt.
Cont straight until Sleeve measures 22 (27)cm/8¾ (10¾)in from beg, ending with a wrong side row. Cast off in patt.

NECKBAND

Join right shoulder seam.
With right side facing and using 3¼mm (No 10/US 3) needles, pick up and k18 (21) sts down left front neck, k centre front sts while dec 2 sts evenly, pick up and k18 (21) sts up right front neck, k back neck sts while dec 4 sts evenly. [80 (94) sts.]
Beg with a p row, work 13 rows in st st.
Cast off loosely.

TO MAKE UP

Join left shoulder and neckband seam, reversing seam on neckband. Sew on sleeves, placing centre of sleeves to shoulder seams. Join side and sleeve seams.

Cabled Rib Sweater

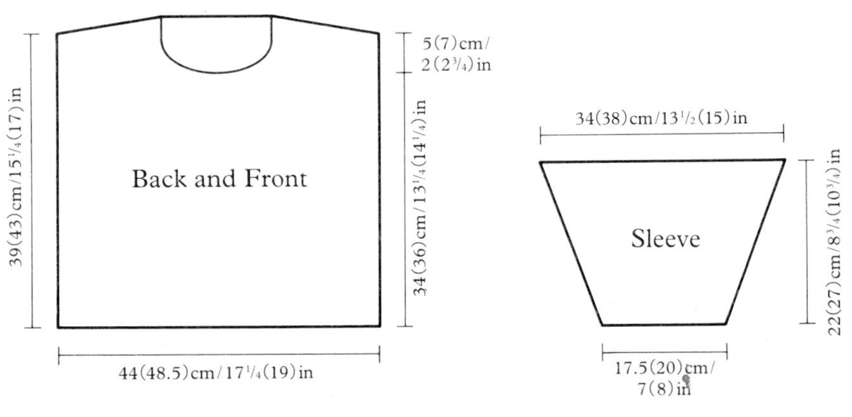
5(7)cm/
2(2¾)in
39(43)cm/15¼(17)in
Back and Front
34(36)cm/13¼(14¼)in
44(48.5)cm/17¼(19)in
34(38)cm/13½(15)in
Sleeve
22(27)cm/8¾(10¾)in
17.5(20)cm/
7(8)in

Vertical Stripe Sweater page 14

MATERIALS

4 (5:6) x 50g balls of Rowan DK
Handknit Cotton each in Blue (A) and
Flame (B).
1 ball in Gold (C).
1 pair each of 3¼mm (No 10/US 3),
3¾mm (No 9/US 5) and 4mm (No 8/US
6) knitting needles.

MEASUREMENTS

To fit age	2-3	3-4	4-5	years
Actual chest	76	83	89	cm
measurement	30	32¾	35	in
Length	38	42	46	cm
	15	16½	18	in
Sleeve seam	24	27	30	cm
	9½	10½	12	in

TENSION

26 sts and 54 rows to 10cm/4in square
over pattern on 4mm (No 8/US 6)
needles.

ABBREVIATIONS

See page 44.

BACK

With 3¾mm (No 9/US 5) needles and A,
cast on 100 (108:116) sts.
** P 1 row.
1st row (right side): With C, k1, sl 2, [k2,
sl 2] to last st, k1.
2nd row: With C, k1, yf, sl 2, [p2, sl 2] to
last st, k1.
3rd row: With A, k3, [sl 2, k2] to last st,
k1.
4th row: With A, k1, p2, [sl 2, p2] to last
st, k1.
These 4 rows form patt. Rep these 4 rows
once more. **
Change to 4mm (No 8/US 6) needles.
Using B instead of C, cont in patt until
Back measures 38 (42:46)cm/15
(16½:18)in from beg, ending with a 4th
patt row.
Shape Shoulders
Cast off 15 (17:18) sts at beg of next 2 rows
and 16 (17:19) sts at beg of foll 2 rows.
Leave rem 38 (40:42) sts on a holder.

FRONT

Work as given for Back until Front
measures 32 (36:40)cm/12¾ (14¼:15¾)in
from beg, ending with a 4th patt row.
Shape Neck
Next row: Patt 42 (45:48), turn.
Work on this set of sts only. Keeping patt
correct, dec 1 st at neck edge on every alt
row until 31 (34:37) sts rem. Cont straight
until Front measures same as Back to
shoulder shaping, ending at side edge.
Shape Shoulder
Cast off 15 (17:18) sts at beg of next row.
Work 1 row. Cast off rem 16 (17:19) sts.
With right side facing, slip centre 16
(18:20) sts on to a holder, rejoin yarn to
rem sts and patt to end. Complete as given
for first side.

SLEEVES

With 3¼mm (No 10/US 3) needles and A,
cast on 40 (44:48) sts.
Work as given for Back from ** to **.
Change to 4mm (No 8/US 6) needles.
Using B instead of C, cont in patt, inc 1 st
at each end of every foll 4th (5th:5th) row
until there are 86 (92:96) sts, working inc
sts into patt. Cont straight until Sleeve
measures 24 (27:30)cm/9½ (10½:12)in
from beg, ending with a 4th patt row.
Cast off.

NECKBAND

Join right shoulder seam.
With right side facing and using 3¼mm
(No 10/US 3) needles and A, pick up and
k17 (16:17) sts down left front neck, k
centre front neck sts, pick up and k17
(15:17) sts up right front neck, k back ne
sts, working twice in last st on **2nd size**
only. [88 (90:96) sts.]
1st row: K0 (2:2)A, Ayf, [p2C, Ayb, k2A
Ayf] to last 0 (0:2) sts, p0 (0:2)C.
2nd row: K0 (0:2)C, [Ayf, p2A, Ayb, k2
to last 0 (2:2) sts, Ayf, p0 (2:2)A.
Rep last 2 rows twice more. Change to
4mm (No 8/US 6) needles. With A, p 1
row, k 1 row. Cast off loosely purlwise.

TO MAKE UP

Join left shoulder and neckband seam. Se
on sleeves, placing centre of sleeves to
shoulder seams. Join side and sleeve seam

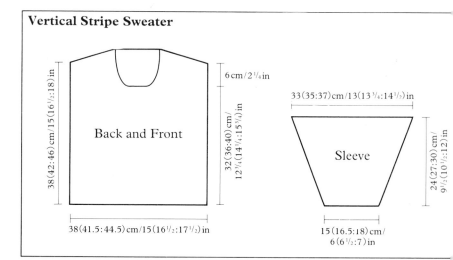

Vertical Stripe Sweater

Back and Front

38 (42:46) cm/15 (16½:18) in

32 (36:40) cm/12¾ (14¼:15¾) in

6 cm/2¼ in

38 (41.5:44.5) cm/15 (16½:17½) in

Sleeve

33 (35:37) cm/13 (13¾:14½) in

24 (27:30) cm/9½ (10½:12) in

15 (16.5:18) cm/6 (6½:7) in

Floral and Fair Isle Cardigan

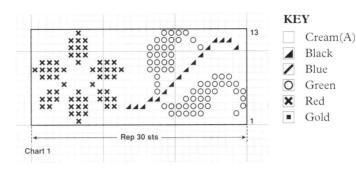

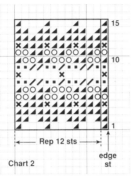

Chart 1 — Rep 30 sts

Chart 2 — Rep 12 sts — edge st

ATERIALS
x 50g balls of Rowan DK Handknit
otton in Cream (A).
balls in Black.
ball each in Blue, Green, Red and
old.
pair each of 3¼mm (No 10/US 3) and
nm (No 8/US 6) knitting needles.
buttons.

EASUREMENTS

o fit age	3–5	years
ctual chest	80	cm
easurement	31½	in
ength	37	cm
	14½	in
eeve seam	29	cm
	11½	in

ENSION
2 sts and 26 rows to 10cm/4in square
ver pattern on 4mm (No 8/US 6)
eedles.

BBREVIATIONS
e page 44.

OTE
hen working in pattern from chart 1,
e separate lengths of contrast yarn for
ch coloured area, twisting yarns
gether on wrong side at joins to avoid
les. Strand yarn not in use loosely
cross wrong side when working in
attern from chart 2 to keep fabric
astic.

BACK AND FRONTS
Worked in one piece to armholes.
With 3¼mm (No 10/US 3) needles and A,
cast on 168 sts.
Beg with a k row, work 4 rows in st st.
Next row (right side): K3, [p2, k2] to last
5 sts, p2, k3.
Next row: P3, [k2, p2] to last 5 sts, k2, p3.
Rep last 2 rows 3 times more, inc 1 st at
centre of last row. [169 sts.]
Change to 4mm (No 8/US 6) needles.
1st row: With A, k.
2nd row: With A, p.
3rd row: K1A, [1 Blue, 1A] to end.
4th row: P1 Blue, [1A, 1 Blue] to end.
5th and 6th rows: As 1st and 2nd rows.
7th row: K1A, reading chart from right to
left, p across 30 sts of 1st row of chart 1
three times, reading chart from left to right,
k across last 17 sts of 1st row of chart 1,
then k across 30 sts twice, k1A.
8th row: P1A, reading chart from right to
left, p across 30 sts of 2nd row of chart 1
three times, reading chart from left to right,
p across last 17 sts of 2nd row of chart 1,
then p across 30 sts twice, p1A.
9th to 19th rows: Rep 7th and 8th rows 5
times, then work 7th row again but working
3rd to 13th rows of chart 1.

20th row: With A, p.
21st row: With A, k.
22nd row: P1A, [1 Blue, 1A] to end.
23rd row: K1 Blue, [1A, 1 Blue] to end.
24th and 25th rows: As 20th and 21st
rows.
26th row: Reading chart from left to right,
[p across 12 sts of 1st row of chart 2] to last
st, p1A, p edge st.
27th row: Reading chart from right to left,
k edge st of 2nd row of chart 2, [k across 12
sts] to end.
28th to 40th rows: Rep 26th and 27th
rows 6 times, then work 26th row again but
working 3rd to 15th rows of chart 2.
These 40 rows form patt. Work a further 4
rows.
Divide for Armholes
Next row: Patt 42, turn.
Work on this set of sts only for Right Front.
Patt 5 rows.
Shape Neck
Keeping patt correct, dec 1 st at beg of next
row and every foll alt row until 26 sts rem.
Patt 3 rows. Cont in A only, work 3 rows.
Shape Shoulder
Cast off 13 sts at beg of next row. Work 1
row. Cast off rem 13 sts.
With right side facing, rejoin yarn to rem

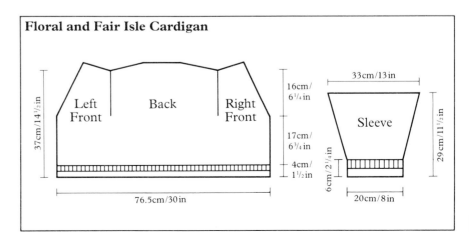

Floral and Fair Isle Cardigan

Left Front — Back — Right Front

37cm/14½in

76.5cm/30in

16cm/6¼in
17cm/6¾in
4cm/1½in

Sleeve

33cm/13in
29cm/11½in
6cm/2½in
20cm/8in

sts, patt 85, turn. Work on this set of sts only for Back. Cont straight until Back matches Right Front to shoulder shaping, ending with a wrong side row.

Shape Shoulders

Cast off 13 sts at beg of next 4 rows. Leave rem 33 sts on a holder.

With right side facing, rejoin yarn to rem sts for Left Front, patt to end. Complete to match Right Front, reversing shapings.

SLEEVES

With 3¼mm (No 10/US 3) needles and A, cast on 38 sts. Beg with a k row, work 4 rows in st st.

Next row (right side): K2, [p2, k2] to end.

Next row: P2, [k2, p2] to end.

Rep last 2 rows 6 times more, then work first of the 2 rows again.

Inc row: Rib 3, [inc in next st, rib 4] to end. [45 sts.]

Change to 4mm (No 8/US 6) needles.

1st to 6th rows: Work as 1st to 6th rows of patt as given for Back and Fronts, inc 1 st at each end of 3rd and 6th rows. [49 sts.]

7th row: K1A, reading chart from right to left, k across 30 sts of 1st row of chart 1, reading chart from left to right k across last 17 sts of 1st row of chart 1, k1A.

8th row: P1A, reading chart from right to left, p across first 17 sts of 2nd row of chart 1, reading chart from left to right, p across 30 sts of 2nd row of chart 1, p1A.

Working from chart 1 as set, cont in patt as given for Back and Fronts, inc 1 st at each end of next row and every foll 3rd row until there are 73 sts, working inc sts into patt. Patt 18 rows straight. Cast off.

FRONT BAND

Join shoulder seams.

With right side facing, using 3¼mm (No 10/US 3) needles and A, pick up and k44 sts up straight edge of Right Front omitting rolled up edge, 40 sts along shaped edge to shoulder, k back neck sts, inc 1 st at centre, pick up and k40 sts down shaped edge of Left Front to beg of neck shaping and 44 sts along straight edge omitting rolled up edge. [202 sts.] Beg with a 2nd row, work 3 rows in rib as given for Sleeves.

Buttonhole row: Rib 4, [yon, k2 tog, rib 10] 4 times, rib to end.

Rib 3 rows. Beg with a k row, work 4 rows in st st. Cast off.

TO MAKE UP

With Gold, embroider bobble at centre of each flower. Sew in sleeves, placing centre of sleeves to shoulder seams. Join sleeve seams. Sew on buttons.

Sampler Cardigan page 16

MATERIALS

7 x 50g balls of Rowan DK Handknit Cotton in Blue (A).
2 balls in Cream (B).
1 ball each in Green, Pink and Rust.
1 pair each of 3¾mm (No 9/US 5) and 4mm (No 8/US 6) knitting needles.
5 buttons.

MEASUREMENTS

To fit age	3–5	years
Actual chest measurement	85	cm
	33½	in
Length	38	cm
	15	in
Sleeve seam	31	cm
	12¼	in

TENSION

20 sts and 28 rows to 10cm/4in square over st st on 4mm (No 8/US 6) needles.

ABBREVIATIONS

See page 44.

NOTE

Read chart from right to left on right side rows and from left to right on wrong side rows. When working in pattern, use separate lengths of yarn for each coloured area and twist yarns together on wrong side at joins to avoid holes.

LEFT FRONT

With 3¾mm (No 9/US 5) needles and A, cast on 43 sts.

1st row: P1, [k1, p1] to end.

This row forms moss st. Rep last row 6 times more.

Inc row: Moss st 10, m1, moss st 7, m1, moss st 13, m1, moss st 7, m1, moss st 6. [47 sts.]

Change to 4mm (No 8/US 6) needles.

Using separate small ball of A at front edge for front band, work in patt from chart as follows:

1st row (right side): K1B, work across 1 row of chart, with A, moss st 5.

2nd row: With A, moss st 5, work across 2nd row of chart, p1B.

These 2 rows set patt. Cont in patt until 85th row of chart has been worked.

Shape Neck

Next row: Moss st 5 and slip these 5 sts on to a safety pin, patt to end.

Patt 1 row. Keeping patt correct, cast off 4 sts at beg of next row and 3 sts at beg of foll alt row. Dec 1 st at neck edge on every row until 27 sts rem. Patt 4 rows straight.

Shape Shoulder

Cast off 14 sts at beg of next row. Work 1 row. Cast off rem 13 sts.

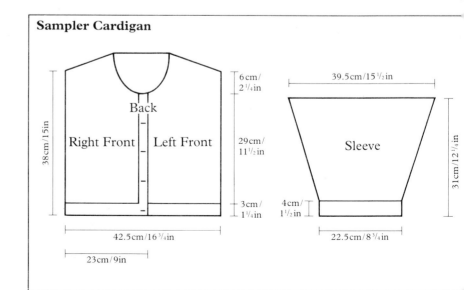

Sampler Cardigan

Back
Right Front   Left Front

38cm/15in
6cm/ 2¼in
29cm/ 11½in
3cm/ 1¼in
42.5cm/16¾in
23cm/9in

39.5cm/15½in
Sleeve
31cm/12¼in
4cm/ 1½in
22.5cm/8¾in

RIGHT FRONT

With 3¾mm (No 9/US 5) needles and A,
cast on 43 sts. Work 6 rows in moss st as
given for Left Front welt.

Buttonhole row (right side): Patt 1, k2
tog, yf, patt to end.

Inc row: Moss st 6, m1, moss st 7, m1,
moss st 13, m1, moss st 7, m1, moss st 10.
[47 sts.]

Change to 4mm (No 8/US 6) needles.
Work in patt from chart as follows:

1st row: With A, moss 5, work across 1st
row of chart, k1B.

2nd row: P1B, work across 2nd row of
chart, with A, moss st 5.

Complete to match Left Front, reversing
shapings and working buttonholes as before
on 19th row and 2 foll 22nd rows.

BACK

With 3¾mm (No 9/US 5) needles and A,
cast on 81 sts. Work 7 rows in moss st as
given for Left Front welt.

Inc row: Moss st 17, [m1, moss st 16] 4
times. [85 sts.]

Change to 4mm (No 8/US 6) needles.
Beg with a k row, work in st st until Back
measures same as Left Front to shoulder
shaping, ending with a wrong side row.

Shape Shoulders

Cast off 14 sts at beg of next 2 rows and 13
sts at beg of foll 2 rows. Leave rem 31 sts
on a holder.

SLEEVES

With 3¾mm (No 9/US 5) needles and A,
cast on 37 sts. Work 11 rows in moss st as
given for Left Front welt.

Inc row: Moss st 5, [m1, moss st 4] to end.
[45 sts.]

Change to 4mm (No 8/US 6) needles.
Beg with a k row, work in st st, inc 1 st at
each end of 5 foll 3rd rows, then on every
foll 4th row until there are 79 sts. Cont
straight until Sleeve measures 32cm/12¼in
from beg, ending with a p row. Cast off.

NECKBAND

Join shoulder seams.

With right side facing, using 3¾mm (No
9/US 5) needles and A, slip sts from Right
Front safety pin on to needle, pick up and
k24 sts up right front neck, k back neck sts,
pick up and k24 sts down left front neck,
then moss st across sts on Left Front safety
pin. [89 sts.] Work 6 rows in moss st,
making buttonhole as before on 2nd row.
Cast off in moss st.

TO MAKE UP

With A, work cross stitch along vertical and
horizontal moss st sections on fronts. Sew
in sleeves, placing centre of sleeves to
shoulder seams. Join side and sleeve seams.
Sew on buttons.

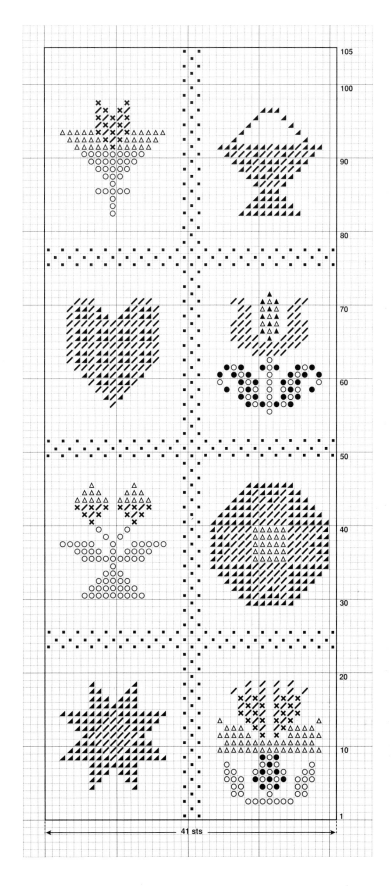

KEY

◢	Blue (A)	
☐	Cream (B)	k on right side and p on wrong side
O	Green	
⁄	Rust	
△	Pink	

▪	Cream (B)	
●	Green	p on right side and k on wrong side
✖	Rust	
▲	Pink	

Rugby Shirt page 17

MATERIALS

5 (6) x 50g balls of Rowan DK Handknit
Cotton in Red (A).
4 (5) balls in Gold (B).
1 ball in White (C).
1 pair each of 3¼mm (No 10/US 3) and
4mm (No 8/US 6) knitting needles.
3 buttons.

MEASUREMENTS

To fit age	2-4	4-6	years
Actual chest	80	88	cm
measurement	31½	34½	in
Length	46	52	cm
	18¼	20½	in
Sleeve seam	25	30	cm
	10	12	in

TENSION

20 sts and 28 rows to 10cm/4in square
over st st on 4mm (No 8/US 6) needles.

ABBREVIATIONS

See page 44.

BACK

With 3¼mm (No 10/US 3) needles and A,
cast on 73 (81) sts.
1st row (right side): P1, [k1, p1] to end.
2nd row: K1, [p1, k1] to end.
Rep last 2 rows 3 times more, inc 1 st at
centre of last row. [74 (82) sts.]
Change to 4mm (No 8/US 6) needles.
Next row: Cast on 3, k to end.
Next row: Cast on 3, p to end. [80 (88)
sts.]
Beg with a k row, work 2 rows in st st.
Cont in st st and stripe patt of 12 rows B
and 12 rows A until Back measures 46
(52)cm/18¼ (20½)in from beg, ending with
a wrong side row.
Shape Shoulders
Cast off 13 (15) sts at beg of next 2 rows
and 13 (14) sts at beg of foll 2 rows. Leave
rem 28 (30) sts on a holder.

FRONT

Work as given for Back until Front
measures 31 (37)cm/12¼ (14½)in from
beg, ending with a wrong side row.
Divide for Opening
Next row: K38 (42), turn.
Work on this set of sts only until Front
measures 41 (47)cm/16¼ (18½)in from
beg, ending at inside edge.
Shape Neck
Cast off 4 (5) sts at beg of next row and 3
sts at beg of foll alt row. Dec 1 st at neck
edge on every row until 26 (29) sts rem.
Cont straight until Front matches Back to
shoulder shaping, ending at side edge.
Shape Shoulder
Cast off 13 (15) sts at beg of next row.
Work 1 row. Cast off rem 13 (14) sts.
With right side facing, rejoin yarn to rem
sts, cast off centre 4 sts, k to end. Complete
as given for first side.

SLEEVES

With 3¼mm (No 10/US 3) needles and A,
cast on 35 (39) sts. Work 5cm/2in in rib as
given for Back welt, ending with a right side
row.
Inc row: Rib 2 (4), [m1, rib 5] 6 times,
m1, rib 3 (5). [42 (46) sts.]
Change to 4mm (No 8/US 6) needles.
Beg with a k row, work in st st and stripe
patt of 12 rows B and 12 rows A, **at the
same time,** inc 1 st at each end of every

foll 3rd (4th) row until there are 70 (74)
sts. Cont straight until Sleeve measures 2⁵
(30)cm/10 (12)in from beg, ending with a
wrong side row. Cast off.

COLLAR

Join shoulder seams.
With right side facing, using 3¼mm (No
10/US 3) needles and C, pick up and k22
(24) sts up right front neck, k back neck st
pick up and k22 (24) sts down left front
neck. [72 (78) sts.]
Inc row: K1, [p1, k1] 5 (6) times, * [p1,
k1] all in next st, [p1, k1] twice; rep from
10 times more, [p1, k1] to end. [83 (89)
sts.]
Beg with a 1st row, work 9 rows in rib as
given for Back welt.
Change to 4mm (No 8/US 6) needles.
Rib 10 rows. Cast off loosely in rib.

BUTTONHOLE BAND

With right side facing, using 3¼mm (No
10/US 3) needles and C, pick up and k27
sts along right edge of opening omitting
Collar. Beg with a 2nd row, work 3 rows i
rib as given for Back welt.
Buttonhole row: [Rib 6, yf, k2 tog] 3
times, rib 3.
Rib 3 rows. Cast off in rib.

BUTTON BAND

With right side facing, using 3¼mm (No
10/US 3) needles and C, pick up and k27
sts along left edge of opening omitting
Collar. Beg with a 2nd row, work 7 rows i
rib as given for Back welt. Cast off in rib.

SIDE EDGINGS

With right side facing, using 3¼mm (No
10/US 3) needles and A, pick up and k 9 s
along row end edge of welt. Beg with a 2n
row, work 3 rows in rib as given for Back
welt. Cast off in rib.

TO MAKE UP

Sew on sleeves, placing centre of sleeves t
shoulder seams. Overlap buttonhole band
over button band and catch down row en
edges at base of opening. Sew row end
edges of side edgings to cast on sts above
welt. Beginning above welt, join side seam
then sleeve seams. Sew on buttons.

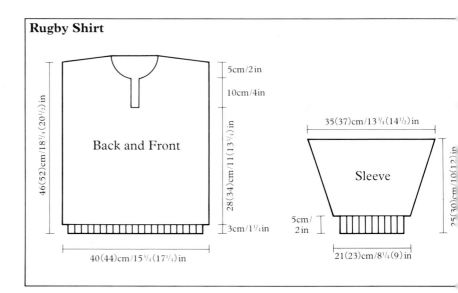

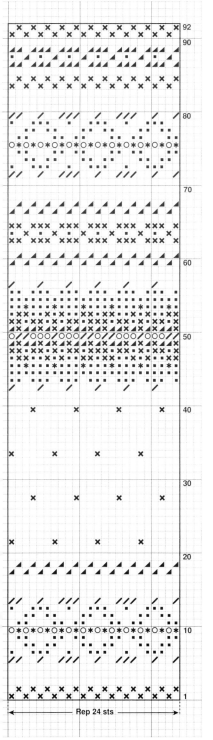

KEY

Navy (A)
Red
Green
Yellow
White
Purple
Pale Blue

MATERIALS

5 x 50g balls of Rowan Designer DK
Wool in Navy (A).
2 balls in Red.
1 ball each in Green, Yellow, White,
Purple and Pale Blue.
1 pair each of 3¼mm (No 10/US 3) and
4mm (No 8/US 6) knitting needles.
1 each of 3¼mm (No 10/US 3) and 4mm
(No 8/US 6) circular knitting needles.
4 buttons.

MEASUREMENTS

To fit age	2–4	years
Actual chest measurement	75	cm
	29½	in
Length	44	cm
	17¼	in
Sleeve seam	31	cm
	12¼	in

TENSION

26 sts and 26 rows to 10cm/4in square
over pattern on 4mm (No 8/US 6)
needles.

ABBREVIATIONS

See page 44.

NOTE

Read chart from right to left on right side
(k) rows and from left to right on wrong
side (p) rows. When working in pattern,
strand yarn not in use loosely across
wrong side to keep fabric elastic.

BACK AND FRONTS

Worked in one piece to armholes.
With 3¼mm (No 10/US 3) circular needle
and A, cast on 187 sts.
Work forwards and backwards in rows. Beg
with a k row, work 6 rows in st st.
Next 2 rows: Cast on 14 sts, k to end. [215
sts.]

Change to 4mm (No 8/US 6) circular
needle.
Beg with a k row, work 2 rows in st st.
Using separate small ball of A yarn at each
end for facings, and twisting yarns together
on wrong side at joins to avoid holes, work
in st st and patt as follows:
1st row (right side): K7A, work across
last 5 sts of 1st row of chart, then rep 24 sts
to last 11 sts, work across first 4 sts, k7A.
2nd row: P7A, work across last 4 sts of
2nd row of chart, then rep 24 sts to last 12
sts, work across first 5 sts, p7A.
These 2 rows set patt. Patt 22 rows.
1st buttonhole row: Patt 1, *work 2 tog,
yrn twice, work 2 tog tbl*, patt 4, rep from
* to *, patt to end.
2nd buttonhole row: Patt to end, working
twice into 'yrn twice' of previous row.
Patt 8 rows. Rep last 10 rows 2 times more,
then rep the 2 buttonhole rows again.
Shape Collar
Next row: Work across last 12 sts of 57th
row of chart, then rep 24 sts to last 11 sts,
work across first 11 sts.
Next row: Work across last 11 sts of 58th
row of chart, then rep 24 sts to last 12 sts,
work across first 12 sts.
Next row: Inc in first st, patt 9, inc in next
st, patt as set to last 11 sts, inc in next st,
patt 9, inc in last st.
Keeping main part in patt as set and
working inc sts into collar patt, patt 1 row.
Next row: Inc in first st, patt to last st, inc
in last st.
Patt 1 row.
Next row: Inc in first st, patt 12, inc in
next st, patt to last 14 sts, inc in next st,
patt 12, inc in last st.
Patt 1 row.
Next row: Inc in first st, patt to last st, inc
in last st.
Patt 1 row.
Next row: Inc in first st, patt 15, inc in
next st, patt to last 17 sts, inc in next st,
patt 15, inc in last st.
Patt 1 row.
Next row: Inc in first st, patt to last st, inc
in last st. [233 sts.]
Patt 1 row.
Divide for Armholes
Next row: Inc in first st, patt 18, inc in
next st, patt 47, inc in next st, turn. [71
sts.]
Work on this set of sts only for Right Front.
Inc at collar edge as set before 1 st at inside
edge on 4 foll 4th rows and at outside edge
on every alt row. [83 sts.] Cont inc at
outside edge only until there are 92 sts, beg
rep of patt with 41st row when the chart
has been completed. Patt 10 rows straight.
Shape Shoulder
Cast off 15 sts at beg of next row and foll
alt row. Cont in A only on rem 62 sts for
back collar. Work 6 rows.
Shape Collar
1st row: Sl 1, k to last 7 sts, yf, sl 1, yb,
turn.
2nd row: Sl 1, p to last 7 sts, yb, sl 1, yf,
turn.
3rd row: Sl 1, k to last 14 sts, yf, sl 1, yb,
turn.
4th row: Sl 1, p to last 14 sts, yb, sl 1, yf,
turn.
5th row: Sl 1, k to last 21 sts, yf, sl 1, yb,
turn.
6th row: Sl 1, p to last 21 sts, yb, sl 1, yf,
turn.

7th row: Sl 1, k to last 28 sts, yf, sl 1, yb, turn.
8th row: Sl 1, p to last 28 sts, yb, sl 1, yf, turn.
Sl 1, k to end. Work 3 rows across all sts.
Next 2 rows: As 7th and 8th rows.
Next 2 rows: As 5th and 6th rows.
Next 2 rows: As 3rd and 4th rows.
Next 2 rows: As 1st and 2nd rows.
Sl 1, k to end. Cont straight until short edge of collar measures 7.5cm/3in, ending with a p row. Leave these sts on a spare needle.
With right side facing, rejoin yarn at armhole edge to rem sts, patt 97 and turn. Work on this set of sts only for Back. Patt 43 rows, beg rep of patt with 41st row when the chart has been completed.

Shape Shoulders
Cast off 15 sts at beg of next 4 rows. Cast off rem 37 sts.
With right side facing, rejoin yarn to rem sts, inc in first st, patt 47, inc in next st, patt 18, inc in last st. Work on this set of 71 sts for Right Front. Complete as given for Left Front, reversing shapings.
With right sides of back collar pieces together and taking 1 st from each needle and working them tog, cast off.

SLEEVES
With 3¼mm (No 10/US 3) needles and A, cast on 49 sts.
Beg with a k row, work 7 rows in st st.
K 1 row for folding line.

Shawl-collared Fair Isle Jacket

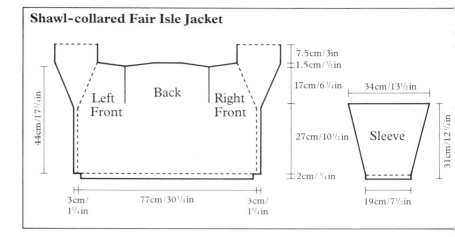

Change to 4mm (No 8/US 6) needles.
Beg with a k row, work 2 rows in st st.
1st row (right side): K last st of 1st row of chart, k across 24 sts twice.
2nd row: P across 24 sts of 2nd row of chart twice, then p first st.
These 2 rows set patt. Work 3rd to 42nd rows of chart as set, inc 1 st at each end of 7th row and 11 foll 3rd rows, working inc sts into patt. [73 sts.] Now work 31st to 70th rows of chart, inc 1 st at each end of 8 foll 4th rows, working inc sts into patt. [89 sts.] Cast off.

TO MAKE UP
Join shoulder seams. Sew in sleeves, placing centre of sleeves to shoulder seams. Join sleeve seams. Turn hems at folding line to wrong side at lower edges of sleeves and back and fronts and slip stitch in place. Sew inner edge of back collar to back neck. Fold facing and collar to wrong side and slip stitch in place, then catch down open end at lower edges. Neaten buttonholes. Sew buttons.

Aran Coat page 21

MATERIALS
8 x 100g hanks of Rowan Magpie Aran.
1 pair each of 4mm (No 8/US 6) and 5mm (No 6/US 8) knitting needles.
Cable needle.
Crochet hook.
12 buttons.

MEASUREMENTS

To fit age	4–6	years
Actual chest measurement	92 36	cm in
Length	51 20	cm in
Sleeve seam	31 12¼	cm in

TENSION
26 sts and 25 rows to 10cm/4in square over panel pattern on 5mm (No 6/US 8) needles.

ABBREVIATIONS
Cr3L = sl next 2 sts on to cable needle and leave at front of work, p1, then k2 from cable needle;
Cr3R = sl next st on to cable needle and leave at back of work, k2, then p1 from cable needle;
C4B = sl next 2 sts on to cable needle and leave at back of work, k2, then k2 from cable needle;
C4F = sl next 2 sts on to cable needle

and leave at front of work, k2, then k2 from cable needle;
Tw4L = sl next 3 sts on to cable needle and leave at front of work, p1, then k1, p1, k1 from cable needle;
Tw4R = sl next st on to cable needle and leave at back of work, k1, p1, k1, then p1 from cable needle.
Also see page 44.

PANEL A
Worked over 12 sts.
1st row (wrong side): K3, p1, k1, p2, k1 p1, k3.
2nd row: P3, sl next 3 sts on to cable needle and leave at front of work, k1, p1, k1, then k1, p1, k1 from cable needle, p3.
3rd row: As 1st row.
4th row: P3, k1, p1, k2, p1, k1, p3.
5th to 7th rows: Work 1st to 3rd rows.
8th row: P2, Tw4R, Tw4L, p2.
9th row: K2, [p1, k1, p1, k2] twice.
10th row: P2, [k1, p1, k1, p2] twice.
11th to 17th rows: Rep 9th and 10th rows 3 times, then work 9th row again.
18th row: P2, Tw4L, Tw4R, p2.
These 18 rows form patt.

PANEL B
Worked over 24 sts.
1st row (wrong side): P1, k5, p4, k4, p4 k5, p1.
2nd row: K1 tbl, p5, C4B, p4, C4F, p5, tbl.
3rd row: As 1st row.
4th row: K1 tbl, p4, Cr3R, Cr3L, p2, Cr3R, Cr3L, p4, k1 tbl.
5th row: P1, k4, p2, [k2, p2] 3 times, k4, p1.
6th row: K1 tbl, p3, [Cr3R, p2, Cr3L] twice, p3, k1 tbl.
7th row: P1, k3, p2, k4, p4, k4, p2, k3, p
8th row: K1 tbl, p3, k2, p4, C4B, p4, p3, k1 tbl.
9th row: As 7th row.
10th row: K1 tbl, p3, k2, p4, k4, p4, k2, p3, k1 tbl.
11th to 13th rows: Work 7th to 9th rows
14th row: K1 tbl, p3, [Cr3L, p2, Cr3R] twice, p3, k1 tbl.
15th row: As 5th row.

th row: K1 tbl, p4, Cr3L, Cr3R, p2,
 [C]r3L, Cr3R, p4, k1 tbl.
[?]th to 21st rows: Work 1st to 5th rows.
[2]nd row: K1 tbl, p4, [k2, p2] twice, k2, sl
[next] 6 sts worked on to cable needle, wrap
[ya]rn anti-clockwise 4 times round these 6
[st]s, then sl these 6 sts on to right hand
[ne]edle, p2, k2, p4, k1 tbl.
[2]3rd row: As 5th row.
[2]4th row: As 16th row.
[T]hese 24 rows form patt.

[P]ANEL C

[W]orked over 12 sts.
[1]st row (wrong side): K3, p1, k1, p2, k1,
[p]1, k3.
[2]nd row: P3, sl next 3 sts on to cable
[n]eedle and leave at back of work, k1, p1,
[k1], then k1, p1, k1 from cable needle, p3.
[3r]d row: As 1st row.
[4t]h row: P3, k1, p1, k2, p1, k1, p3.
[5t]h to 7th rows: Work 1st to 3rd rows.
[8t]h row: P2, Tw4R, Tw4L, p2.
[9t]h row: K2, [p1, k1, k2] twice.
[10t]h row: P2, [k1, p1, k1, p2] twice.
[11t]h to 17th rows: Rep 9th and 10th rows
[3] times, then work 9th row again.
[18]th row: P2, Tw4L, Tw4R, p2.
[T]hese 18 rows form patt.

[B]ACK

[W]ith 4mm (No 8/US 6) needles, cast on 95
[st]s.
[1]st row: P1, [k1, p1] to end.
[T]his row forms moss st. Rep last row 3
[ti]mes more.
[In]c row: Moss st 7, [m1, moss st 4] 9
[ti]mes, m1, moss st 9, [m1, moss st 4] 9
[ti]mes, m1, moss st 7. [115 sts.]
[C]hange to 5mm (No 6/US 8) needles.
[1]st row (wrong side): Moss st 5, p1, work
[1]st row of panel C, work 1st row of panel
[B], work 1st row of panel C, p1, moss st 5,
[p]1, work 1st row of panel A, work 1st row
[o]f panel B, work 1st row of panel A, p1,
[m]oss st 5.
[2]nd row: Moss st 5, k1 tbl, work 2nd row
[o]f panel A, work 2nd row of panel B, work
[2]nd row of panel A, k1 tbl, moss st 5, k1
[tb]l, work 2nd row of panel C, work 2nd
[ro]w of panel B, work 2nd row of panel C,
[k]1 tbl, moss st 5.
[T]hese 2 rows set patt. Cont in patt until
[B]ack measures 51cm/20in from beg,
[e]nding with a wrong side row.
[S]hape Shoulders
[C]ast off 20 sts at beg of next 4 rows. Leave
[re]m 35 sts on a holder.

[P]OCKET LININGS (make 2)

[W]ith 5mm (No 6/US 8) needles, cast on 24
[st]s. Work 1st to 24th rows of panel B, then
[1]st to 4th rows again. Leave sts on a holder.

[L]EFT FRONT

[W]ith 4mm (No 8/US 6) needles, cast on 50
[st]s.
[1]st row: [P1, k1] to end.
[2]nd row: [K1, p1] to end.
[T]hese 2 rows form moss st. Rep last 2 rows
[o]nce more.
[In]c row: Moss st 7, [m1, moss st 2] 3
[ti]mes, m1, moss st 24, m1, [moss st 2, m1]
[3] times, moss st 7. [58 sts.]
[C]hange to 5mm (No 6/US 8) needles.
[1]st row (wrong side): Moss st 5, p1, work
[1]st row of panel A, moss st 22, work 1st
[ro]w of panel A, p1, moss st 5.
[2]nd row: Moss st 5, k1 tbl, work 2nd row
[of] panel A, moss st 22, work 2nd row of
[p]anel A, k1 tbl, moss st 5.
[W]ork a further 25 rows as set.

Place Pocket

Next row: Patt 18, cast off next 22 sts in
moss st, patt to end.
Next row: Patt 18, patt across sts of one
pocket lining, patt to end. [60 sts.]
Cont in patt as set on last row until Front
measures 43cm/17in from beg, ending with
a wrong side row.

Shape Neck

Next row: Patt to last 6 sts, turn; leave the
6 sts on a safety pin.
Keeping patt correct, cast off 3 sts at beg of
next row and foll alt row. Dec 1 st at neck
edge on every row until 40 sts rem. Cont
straight until Front measures same as Back
to shoulder shaping, ending with a wrong
side row.

Shape Shoulder

Cast off 20 sts at beg of next row. Work 1
row. Cast off rem 20 sts.
Mark front edge to indicate position of 8
buttons: first one 6 rows up from cast on
edge, last one 2 rows below neck shaping
and rem 6 evenly spaced between.

RIGHT FRONT

With 4mm (No 8/US 6) needles, cast on 50
sts.
1st row: [K1, p1] to end.
2nd row: [P1, k1] to end.
These 2 rows form moss st. Rep last 2 rows
once more.
Inc row: Moss st 7, [m1, moss st 2] 3
times, m1, moss st 24, m1, [moss st 2, m1]
3 times, moss st 7. [58 sts.]
Change to 5mm (No 6/US 8) needles.
1st row (wrong side): Moss st 5, p1, work
1st row of panel C, moss st 22, work 1st
row of panel C, p1, moss st 5.
2nd (buttonhole) row: Moss st 2, yrn, p2
tog, k1, k1 tbl, work 2nd row of panel C,
moss st 22, work 2nd row of panel C, k1
tbl, moss st 5.
Complete as given for Left Front, reversing
shapings and making buttonholes as before
to match markers.

SLEEVES

With 4mm (No 8/US 6) needles, cast on 38
sts. Work 12 rows in k1, p1 rib.
Inc row: Rib 2, [m1, rib 2] to end. [56
sts.]
Change to 5mm (No 6/US 8) needles.
1st row (wrong side): P1, k1, p2, work
1st row of panel C, work 1st row of panel
B, work 1st row of panel A, p2, k1, p1.
2nd row: P1, k1, p1, k1 tbl, work 2nd row
of panel A, work 2nd row of panel B, work
2nd row of panel C, k1 tbl, p1, k1, p1.

These 2 rows set patt. Cont in patt, inc 1 st
at each end of next row and every foll 4th
row until there are 82 sts, working inc sts
into moss st. Cont straight until Sleeve
measures 31cm/12¼in from beg, ending
with a wrong side row. Cast off.

COLLAR

Join shoulder seams.
With right side facing and using 4mm (No
8/US 6) needles, slip 6 sts from Right Front
safety pin on to needle, pick up and k21 sts
up right front neck, k back neck sts, pick up
and k21 sts down left front neck, then moss
st across from Left Front safety pin. [89
sts.] Work 1 row in moss st.
Next 2 rows: Moss st to last 24 sts, turn.
Next 2 rows: Moss st to last 21 sts, turn.
Next 2 rows: Moss st to last 18 sts, turn.
Cont in this way, working 3 sts more at end
of next 6 rows, turn and moss st to end.
Cast off 3 sts at beg of next 2 rows. Work
20 rows in moss st. Cast off loosely in patt.

POCKET FLAPS (make 2)

With 5mm (No 6/US 8) needles, cast on 21
sts. Work 8 rows in moss st as given for
Back welt. Dec 1 st at each end of next row
and 3 foll alt rows.
Buttonhole row: Moss st 6, yf, k2 tog,
moss st 5.
Dec 1 st at each end of next 2 rows. Cast
off in patt.
With right side facing and using crochet
hook, work 1 row of double crochet around
shaped edges, omitting cast on edge. Do
not turn. Work 1 row of backward double
crochet (double crochet worked from left to
right). Fasten off.

BELT

With 4mm (No 8/US 6) needles, cast on 61
sts. Work 9 rows in moss st as given for
Back welt. Cast off in patt.

TO MAKE UP

Sew on sleeves, placing centre of sleeves to
shoulder seams. Join side and sleeve seams.
Catch down pocket linings. Sew pocket
flaps in place. Place belt on back in desired
position and secure ends in place with
buttons. Sew on buttons.

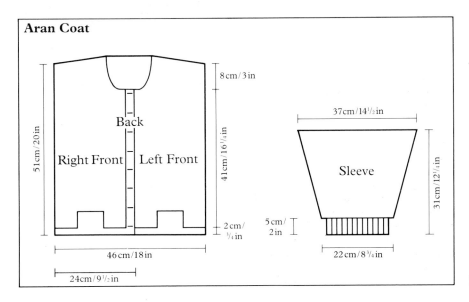

Aran Coat

57

Bird Jacket and Hat page 22

MATERIALS

Jacket: 2 x 50g balls of Rowan DK Handknit Cotton in each of Royal and Sea Green.
1 ball each in Cerise, Orange, Brown, Lime, Cream, Yellow, Jade and Red.
1 pair of 4mm (No 8/US 6) knitting needles.
Medium size crochet hook.
4 buttons.
Hat: 2 x 50g balls of Rowan DK Handknit Cotton in Royal.
1 ball each in Sea Green, Cerise, Orange, Brown, Lime, Cream, Yellow, Jade and Red.
1 pair of 4mm (No 8/US 6) knitting needles.
Medium size crochet hook.

MEASUREMENTS

To fit age	6-12	months
Actual chest measurement	65 25½	cm in
Length	28 11	cm in
Sleeve seam	18 7	cm in

TENSION

20 sts and 28 rows to 10cm/4in square over pattern on 4mm (No 8/US 6) needles.

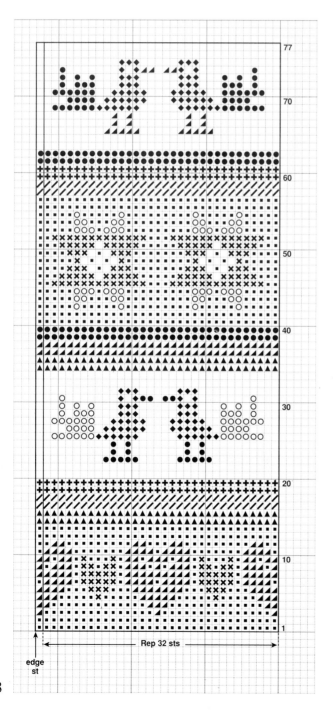

KEY

☐	Royal
▪	Sea Green
◤	Cerise
✖	Orange
▲	Brown
╱	Lime
✚	Cream
●	Yellow
◆	Jade
○	Red

ABBREVIATIONS

ch = chain;
dc = double crochet;
ss = slip stitch.
Also see page 44.

NOTE

Read chart from right to left on right sid(e)
(k) rows and from left to right on wrong
side (p) rows. When working in pattern,
use separate length of yarn for each mot(if)
and twist yarns together on wrong side a(t)
joins to avoid holes.

JACKET

BACK AND FRONTS

Worked in one piece to armholes.
With 4mm (No 8/US 6) needles and Sea
Green, cast on 129 sts. Beg with a k row,
work in st st and patt from chart until 42n(d)
row of chart has been worked.
Divide for Armholes
Next row: Patt 32, turn.
Work on this set of sts only for Right Fron(t)
Patt 9 rows straight.
Shape Neck
Keeping patt correct, dec 1 st at beg of ne(xt)
row and every foll alt row until 19 sts rem.
Cont in Royal only.
Shape Shoulder
Cast off 10 sts at beg of next row. Work 1
row. Cast off rem 9 sts.
With right side facing, rejoin yarn to rem
sts, cast off 1 st, patt until there are 63 sts
on right hand needle, turn. Work on this
set of sts only for Back. Patt 33 rows. Con(t)
in Royal only.
Shape Shoulders
Cast off 10 sts at beg of next 2 rows and 9
sts at beg of foll 2 rows. Cast off rem 25 st(s)
With right side facing, rejoin yarn to rem
sts for Left Front, cast off 1 st, patt to end.
Complete as given for Right Front,
reversing shapings and noting that the last
dec at neck edge is worked on first row of
shoulder shaping.

SLEEVES

With 4mm (No 8/US 6) needles and
Brown, cast on 33 sts. Beg with a k row an(d)

th row of chart, cont in st st and patt
m chart, **at the same time**, inc 1 st at
ch end of 3rd row and every foll 4th row
til there are 53 sts, working inc sts into
t. Patt 9 rows. With Yellow, cast off.

) MAKE UP
n shoulder seams.
rochet Edging
th right side facing, using crochet hook,
yal and beg at centre of lower edge, work
ound of dc along lower edge, front edges
d back neck, working 3 dc in each
ner, ss in first dc.
xt round: 1 ch, 1 dc in each dc, making
uttonhole loops along straight right front
ge by working 2 ch and missing 2 dc, ss
1 ch.
 not turn. Work 1 round of backward dc
worked from left to right). Fasten off.
w in sleeves, placing centre of sleeves to
oulder seams. Join sleeve seams. Work
chet edging along lower edges of sleeves.
w on buttons.

HAT

R FLAPS (make 2)
th 4mm (No 8/US 6) needles and
rise, cast on 6 sts. P 1 row. Beg with a k
w, work in st st and stripes of 2 rows Sea
een, 2 rows Brown, 2 rows Lime, 2 rows
eam, 2 rows Royal, 2 rows Orange, 2
vs Yellow, 2 rows Cerise, 2 rows Sea
een, 2 rows Brown and 2 rows Lime, **at
e same time**, inc 1 st at each end of first
ows, then at each end of 3 foll alt rows.
) sts.] Leave these sts on a holder.

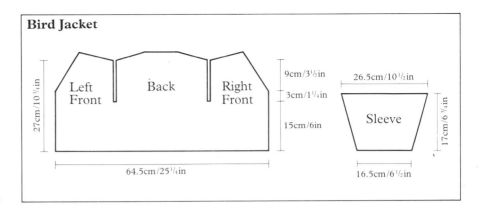

Bird Jacket

MAIN PART
With 4mm (No 8/US 6) needles and Royal,
cast on 13 sts, k these sts, then k across 20
sts of first ear flap, cast on 31 sts, then k
across 20 sts of second ear flap, cast on 13
sts. [97 sts.] P 1 row. Work 2 rows Orange,
2 rows Yellow, 2 rows Cerise, 2 rows Sea
Green, 2 rows Brown, 2 rows Lime and 2
rows Cream.
Now work 21st to 34th rows of chart.
Shape Top
Next row: With Brown, k2, [k2 tog, k3, k2
tog, k2] to last 5 sts, k2 tog, k3. [76 sts.]
Work 1 row Brown, 2 rows Cerise, 2 rows
Yellow, 2 rows Orange and 2 rows Sea
Green.
Next row: With Lime, k1, [k2 tog, k1] to
end. [51 sts.]
Work 1 row Lime, 2 rows Cream and 2
rows Brown.
Next row: With Cerise, k1, [k2 tog] to

end. [26 sts.]
Work 1 row Cerise. Cont in Royal, work 4
rows.
Next row: [K2 tog] to end. [13 sts.]
Work 3 rows.
Next row: K1, [k2 tog] to end. [7 sts.]
Break off yarn, thread end through rem sts,
pull up and secure.

TO MAKE UP
Join back seam. With right side facing,
using crochet hook and Royal, work 1
round of dc around outside edge, working 2
dc together in each corner, ss in first dc. Do
not turn. Work 1 round of backward dc (dc
worked from left to right). Fasten off.

Rose Jacket page 23

page 23

ATERIALS
x 50g balls of Rowan DK Handknit
otton in Gold (A).
ball each in Dark Green, Light Green,
nk, Red and Orange.
pair each of 3¼mm (No 10/US 3) and
m (No 8/US 6) knitting needles.
buttons.

EASUREMENTS

o fit age	2–4	years
ctual chest	79	cm
easurement	31	in
ngth	31	cm
	12¼	in
eeve seam	21	cm
	8¼	in

ENSION
sts and 28 rows to 10cm/4in square
er st st on 4mm (No 8/US 6) needles.

BBREVIATIONS
e page 44.

OTE
hen working in pattern, use separate
ngths of contrast colours for each
loured area and twist yarns together on
rong side at joins to avoid holes.

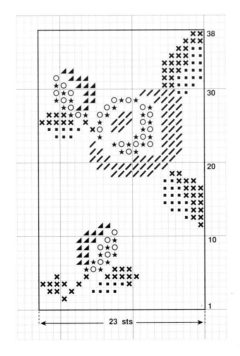

23 sts

KEY

☐	Gold	○	Pink
✖	Dark Green	◢	Red
▪	Light Green	⟋	Orange
★	Pink but p on right side and k on wrong side		

BACK
With 3¼mm (No 10/US 3) needles and A,
cast on 72 sts.
1st row (right side): [K1, p1] to end.
2nd row: [P1, k1] to end.
These 2 rows form moss st. Rep last 2 rows
3 times more.
Change to 4mm (No 8/US 6) needles.
1st row: K7A, reading chart from right to
left, k across 1st row, k12A, reading chart
from left to right, k across 1st row, k7A.
2nd row: P7A, reading chart from right to
left, p across 2nd row, p12A, reading chart
from left to right, p across 2nd row, p7A.
These 2 rows set patt. Cont in patt, noting
that Pink areas are worked in moss st, **at
the same time**, inc 1 st at each end of 5th
row and 3 foll 8th rows, working inc sts in
A. [80 sts.] Patt 9 rows straight.
Shape Armholes
Cast off 4 sts at beg of next 2 rows. [72 sts.]
Patt 34 rows. Cont in A only. Work 2 rows
in st st, then 6 rows in moss st.
Shape Shoulders
Cast off 12 sts at beg of next 4 rows. Leave
rem 24 sts on a holder.

LEFT FRONT
With 3¼mm (No 10/US 3) needles and A,
cast on 38 sts. Work 8 rows in moss st as
given for Back welt.
Change to 4mm (No 8/US 6) needles.
1st row: K7A, reading chart from right to
left, k across 1st row, with A, k3, moss st 5.
2nd row: With A, moss st 5, p3, reading
chart from left to right, p across 2nd row,
p7A.
These 2 rows set patt. Cont in patt, inc 1 st

59

at beg of 5th row and 3 foll 8th rows. [42 sts.] Patt 9 rows straight.

Shape Armhole
Cast off 4 sts at beg of next row. [38 sts.] Patt 29 rows.

Shape Neck
Next row: Patt to last 5 sts, turn; leave the 5 sts on a safety pin.
Cast off 3 sts at beg of next row. Dec 1 st at neck edge on next 4 rows. Cont in A only. Work 2 rows, dec 1 st at neck edge on every row. [24 sts.] Work 6 rows in moss st.

Shape Shoulder
Cast off 12 sts at beg of next row. Work 1 row. Cast off rem 12 sts.
Mark front edge to indicate position of 5 buttons: first on 2 rows up from lower edge, last one 2 rows down from neck shaping and rem 3 evenly spaced between.

RIGHT FRONT
With 3¼mm (No 10/US 3) needles and A, cast on 38 sts. Work 2 rows in moss st as given for Back welt.
Buttonhole row (right side): Moss st 2, k2 tog, yf, k1, patt to end.
Work 5 rows in moss st.
Change to 4mm (No 8/US 6) needles.
1st row: With A, moss st 5, k3, reading chart from left to right, k across 1st row, k7A.
2nd row: P7A, reading chart from right to left, p across 2nd row, with A, p3, moss st 5.
Complete as given for Left Front, reversing shapings and making buttonholes as before to match markers.

SLEEVES
With 3¼mm (No 10/US 3) needles and A, cast on 38 sts. Work 11 rows in moss st as given for Back welt.
Inc row: Moss st 6, [m1, moss st 4] to end. [46 sts.]
Change to 4mm (No 8/US 6) needles.
1st row: Reading chart from right to left, k across last 19 sts of 1st row, k8A, reading chart from left to right, k across first 19 sts of 1st row.
2nd row: Reading chart from right to left, p across last 19 sts of 2nd row, p8A, reading chart from left to right, p across first 19 sts of 2nd row.
These 2 rows set patt. Cont in patt, inc 1 st at each end of 3rd row and every foll 5th row until there are 64 sts, working inc sts into patt. Patt 5 rows. Mark each end of last row. Patt 6 rows. Cast off.

COLLAR
Join shoulder seams.
With right side facing, using 4mm (No 8/US 6) needles and A, slip sts from Right Front safety pin on to needle, pick up and k21 sts up right front neck, work across back neck sts as follows: k2, [m1, k2] 11 times, pick up and k21 sts down left front neck, moss st across sts on safety pin. [87 sts.]
Next row: Moss st 8, k to last 8 sts, moss st 8.
Next row: Cast off 4 sts, moss st 3 sts more, p 57, turn.
Next row: K43, turn.
Next row: P46, turn.
Next row: K49, turn.
Cont in this way, working 3 sts more at end of next 6 rows, turn and p to last 8 sts, moss st 8.
Next row: Cast off 4 sts, moss st 3 sts more, k to last 4 sts, moss st 4.
Next row: Moss st 4, p to last 4 sts, moss st 4.
Next row: Moss st 4, m1, k to last 4 sts, m1, moss st 4.
Next row: Moss st 4, p to last 4 sts, moss st 4.
Next row: Moss st 4, k to last 4 sts, moss st 4.
Rep last 4 rows twice more. Moss st 5 rows across all sts. Cast off loosely in moss st.

STRAPS (make 2)
With 4mm (No 8/US 6) needles and A, cast on 7 sts.
1st row: K1, [p1, k1] to end.
This row forms moss st. Cont in moss st until Strap measures 7cm/2¾in from beg.
Buttonhole row: Moss st 3, yf, k2 tog, moss st 2.
Work 2 rows. Dec 1 st at each end of next rows.
Next row: Sl 1, k2 tog, psso and fasten o[f]

TO MAKE UP
Sew on sleeves, placing centre of sleeves t[o] shoulder seams and sewing rows above markers to cast off sts at armholes. Place straps on top of front welts with cast on edge at side edge and secure in position. Join side and sleeve seams. Sew on butto[ns.]

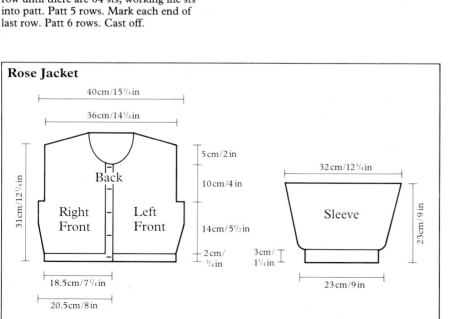

Rose Jacket

40cm/15¾in
36cm/14¼in
31cm/12¼in
Back
Right Front
Left Front
5cm/2in
10cm/4in
14cm/5½in
2cm/¾in
18.5cm/7¼in
20.5cm/8in

32cm/12¾in
Sleeve
3cm/1¼in
23cm/9in
23cm/9in

MATERIALS

x 50g balls of Rowan Cotton Glace.
air of 3mm (No 11/US 2) and 3¼mm
o 10/US 3) knitting needles.
ble needle.

MEASUREMENTS

fit age	3–4	years
tual chest	80	cm
easurement	31½	in
ngth	41	cm
	16	in
eve seam	30	cm
	12	in

TENSION

sts and 34 rows to 10cm/4in square
er st st on 3¼mm (No 10/US 3)
edles.

ABBREVIATIONS

b = [k1, p1, k1, p1, k1] all in next st,
rn, k5, turn, p5] twice, then pass 2nd,
d, 4th and 5th sts over first st;
k = [k1, p1, k1, p1] all in next st, then
ss 2nd, 3rd and 4th sts over first st;
= sl next st on to cable needle and
ve at back of work, k1, then k1 from
le needle;
= sl next 2 sts on to cable needle and
ve at back of work, k2, then k2 from
le needle;
3L = sl next 2 sts on to cable needle
d leave at front of work, p1, then k2
m cable needle;
3R = sl next st on to cable needle and
ve at back of work, k2, then p1 from
le needle.
so see page 44.

PANEL A

orked over 12 sts.
row (right side): P3, sl next st on to
le needle and leave at back of work, k2,
n k1 from cable needle, sl next 2 sts on
cable needle and leave at front of work,
, then k2 from cable needle, p3.
d row: K3, p6, k3.
t row: P2, Cr3R, C2, Cr3L, p2.

4th row: K2, p2, [k1, p2] twice, k2.
5th row: P1, Cr3R, p1, C2, p1, Cr3L, p1.
6th row: K1, p2, [k2, p2] twice, k1.
7th row: Cr3R, p2, C2, p2, Cr3L.
8th row: P2, [k3, p2] twice.
9th row: Cr3L, p2, C2, p2, Cr3R.
10th row: As 6th row.
11th row: P1, Cr3L, p1, C2, p1, Cr3R, p1.
12th row: As 4th row.
13th row: P2, Cr3L, C2, Cr3R, p2.
14th row: As 2nd row.
15th row: P3, Cr3L, Cr3R, p3.
16th row: K4, p4, k4.
17th row: P4, k4, p4.
18th row: As 16th row.
These 18 rows form patt.

PANEL B

Worked over 13 sts.
1st row (right side): K6, p1, k6.
2nd row: P5, k1, p1, k1, p5.
3rd row: K4, p1, [k1, p1] twice, k4.
4th row: P3, k1, [p1, k1] 3 times, p3.
5th row: K2, p1, [k1, p1] 4 times, k2.
6th row: P1, [k1, p1] 6 times.
7th row: As 5th row.
8th row: As 4th row.
9th row: As 3rd row.
10th row: As 2nd row.
11th row: K6, p1, k6.
12th row: P13.
13th row: K13.
14th row: P13.
These 14 rows form patt.

PANEL C

Worked over 16 sts.
1st row (right side): K2, p4, k4, p4, k2.
2nd row: P2, k4, p4, k4, p2.
3rd row: K2, p4, C4, p4, k2.
4th row: As 2nd row.
5th row: [Cr3L, p2, Cr3R] twice.
6th row: K1, [p2, k2] 3 times, p2, k1.
7th row: P1, Cr3L, Cr3R, p2, Cr3L, Cr3R, p1.
8th row: K2, p4, k4, p4, k2.
9th row: P2, C4, p4, C4, p2.
10th row: As 8th row.
11th row: P2, k4, p4, k4, p2.
12th to 18th rows: Work 8th to 11th rows once, then work 8th to 10th rows again.
19th row: P1, Cr3R, Cr3L, p2, Cr3R, Cr3L, p1.
20th row: As 6th row.
21st row: [Cr3R, p2, Cr3L] twice.
22nd to 28th rows: Work 2nd to 4th rows

---

once, then work 1st to 4th rows again.
These 28 rows form patt.

BACK

With 3¼mm (No 10/US 3) needles, cast on 101 sts.
Work border patt as follows:
1st row (wrong side): K.
2nd row: K5, mb, [k9, mb] to last 5 sts, k5.
3rd and 4th rows: K.
5th row: P1, [yrn, p3, p3 tog tbl, p3, yrn, p1] to end.
6th row: K2, [yf, k2, sl 1, k2 tog, psso, k2, yf, k3] to last 9 sts, yf, k2, sl 1, k2 tog, psso, k2, yf, k2.
7th row: P3, [yrn, p1, p3 tog tbl, p1, yrn, p5] to last 8 sts, yrn, p1, p3 tog tbl, p1, yrn, p3.
8th row: K4, [yf, sl 1, k2 tog, psso, yf, k7] to last 7 sts, yf, sl 1, k2 tog, psso, yf, k4.
9th row: P.
Change to 3mm (No 11/US 2) needles and k 4 rows. **
Change to 3¼mm (No 10/US 3) needles.
Inc row: K25, [k twice in next st, k 24] 3 times, k1. [104 sts.]
Beg with a p row, work 20 rows in st st.
Inc row: P12, [p twice in next st, p35, p twice in next st, p6] twice, p6. [108 sts.]
Work in main patt as follows:
1st row: K7, work 1st row of panel A, k7, work 1st row of panel B, k7, work 1st row of panel C, k7, work 1st row of panel B, k7, work 1st row of panel A, k7.
2nd row: K7, work 2nd row of panel A, k7, work 2nd row of panel B, k7, work 2nd row of panel C, k7, work 2nd row of panel B, k7, work 2nd row of panel A, k7.
3rd row: K3, mk, k3, work 3rd row of panel A, k3, mk, k3, work 3rd row of panel B, k3, mk, k3, work 3rd row of panel C, k3, mk, k3, work 3rd row of panel B, k3, mk, k3, work 3rd row of panel A, k3, mk, k3.
4th row: K7, work 4th row of panel A, k7, work 4th row of panel B, k7, work 4th row of panel C, k7, work 4th row of panel B, k7, work 4th row of panel A, k7.
These 4 rows form garter st patt between panels and set position of panels. Cont in patt until Back measures 41cm/16in from points, ending with a right side row.
Shape Shoulder and Neck
Next row: Patt 40, cast off next 28 sts, patt to end.
Work on last set of sts only. Cast off 12 sts at beg of next row, 4 sts at beg of foll row

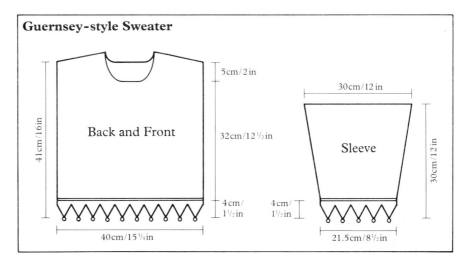

Guernsey-style Sweater

Back and Front
41cm/16in
5cm/2in
32cm/12½in
4cm/1½in
40cm/15¼in

Sleeve
30cm/12in
30cm/12in
4cm/1½in
21.5cm/8½in

and 12 sts at beg of next row. Work 1 row.
Cast off rem 12 sts.
With right side facing, rejoin yarn to rem
sts and patt to end. Complete as given for
first side.

FRONT
Work as given for Back until Front
measures 36cm/14in from points, ending
with a right side row.
Shape Neck
Next row: Patt 45, cast off next 18 sts, patt
to end.
Work on last set of sts only. Keeping patt
correct, dec 1 st at neck edge on next 5
rows, then on 4 foll alt rows. [36 sts.] Cont
straight until Front matches Back to
shoulder shaping, ending at side edge.
Shape Shoulder
Cast off 12 sts at beg of next row and foll
alt row. Work 1 row. Cast off rem 12 sts.
With right side facing, rejoin yarn to rem
sts and complete as given for first side.

SLEEVES
With 3¼mm (No 10/US 3) needles, cast on
51 sts.
Work as given for Back to ★★.
Change to 3¼mm (No 10/US 3) needles.
Inc row: K5, [k twice in next st, k9] 4
times, k twice in next st, k5. [56 sts.]
Beg with a p row, work 12 rows in st st, inc
1 st at each end of 4th row and foll 6th row.
[60 sts.]
Inc row: P26, p twice in next st, p6, p
twice in next st, p26. [62 sts.]
Work in main patt as follows:
1st row: K3, work 1st row of panel B, k7,
work 1st row of panel C, k7, work 1st row
of panel B, k3.
2nd row: K3, work 2nd row of panel B, k7,
work 2nd row of panel C, k7, work 2nd row
of panel B, k3.
3rd row: Inc in 1st st, k2, work 3rd row of
panel B, k3, mk, k3, work 3rd row of panel
C, k3, mk, k3, work 3rd row of panel B, k2,
inc in last st.
4th row: K4, work 4th row of panel B, k7,
work 4th row of panel C, k7, work 4th row
of panel B, k4.
These 4 rows form garter st patt between
panels and set position of panels. Cont in
patt, inc 1 st at each end of 5th row and 2
foll 6th rows, working inc sts into garter st
patt. Inc 1 st at each end of 5 foll 8th rows,
working inc sts into reverse st st. [80 sts.]
Cont straight until Sleeves measure
30cm/12in from points, ending with a
wrong side row. Cast off.

COLLAR
With 3¼mm (No 10/US 3) needles, cast on
131 sts.
Work 1st to 8th rows of border patt as
given for Back.
Next row (wrong side): P3, [p2 tog, p4, p2 tog, p5] 9
times, p2 tog, p4, p2 tog, p3. [111 sts.]
Change to 3mm (No 11/US 2) needles.
K 4 rows.
Next row: K3, [k2 tog, k3, k2 tog, k4] 9
times, k2 tog, k3, k2 tog, k2. [91 sts.]
Next row: P1, [k1, p1] to end.
Next row: K1, [p1, k1] to end.
Rep last 2 rows twice more.
Next row: Rib 6, [work 3 times in next st,
rib 12] 6 times, work 3 times in next st, rib
6. [105 sts.]
Rib 2 rows. Cast off loosely in rib.

TO MAKE UP
Join shoulder seams. Sew on sleeves,
placing centre of sleeves to shoulder seams.
Join side and sleeve seams. Sew cast off
edge of collar to neck edge, beginning and
ending at left shoulder seam. Join collar
together.

Fair Isle Waistcoat page 25

MATERIALS
2 (3:4) x 50g balls of Rowan Cotton
Glace in Red (A).
2 (2:3) balls in Cream.
1 ball each in Green, Purple, Gold and
Turquoise.
1 pair each of 2¾mm (No 12/US 2) and
3¼mm (No 10/US 3) knitting needles.
4 (5:6) buttons.

MEASUREMENTS

To fit age	6–9	12–18	24–36	mont
Actual chest	61	70	79	cm
measurement	24	27½	31	in
Length	24	30.5	37	cm
	9½	12	14½	in

TENSION
28 sts and 32 rows to 10cm/4in square
over pattern on 3¼mm (No 10/US 3)
needles.

ABBREVIATIONS
See page 44.

NOTE
Read chart from right to left on right si
(k) rows and from left to right on wron
side (p) rows. When working in patterr
strand yarn not in use loosely across
wrong side to keep fabric elastic.

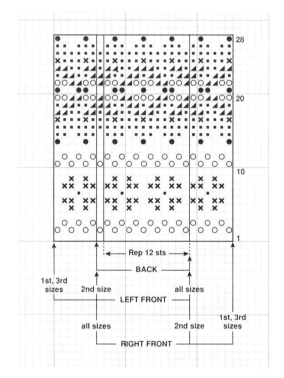

KEY

□	Red(A)
▪	Cream
○	Green
✕	Purple
●	Gold
◢	Turquoise

BACK
With 2¾mm (No 12/US 2) needles and A,
cast on 75 (87:99) sts.
1st row: K1, [p1, k1] to end.
2nd row: P1, [k1, p1] to end.
Rep last 2 rows until welt measures
3cm/1¼in, ending with a 1st row.
Next row (wrong side): Rib 6 (7:9), m1,
[rib 7 (8:9), m1] to last 6 (8:9) sts, rib 6
(8:9). [85 (97:109) sts.]
Change to 3¼mm (No 10/US 3) needles.
Beg with a k row, work in st st and patt
from chart until Back measures 14
(19:24)cm/5½ (7½:9½)in from beg, ending
with a wrong side row.

Shape Armholes
Cast off 5 (6:7) sts at beg of next 2 rows.
Keeping patt correct, dec 1 st at each end
of every row until 59 (65:71) sts rem. Co
straight until armholes measure 10
(11.5:13)cm/4 (4½:5)in, ending with a
wrong side row.
Shape Shoulders
Cast off 7 (8:9) sts at beg of next 4 rows.
Leave rem 31 (33:35) sts on a holder.

LEFT FRONT
With 2¾mm (No 12/US 2) needles and ⸱
cast on 37 (43:49) sts. Beg with a 2nd ro⸱
work in rib as given for Back welt for
3cm/1¼in, ending with a 2nd row.

: row (wrong side): Rib 4, m1, [rib 6 8), m1] to last 3 (4:5) sts, rib 3 (4:5). (49:55) sts.]
ange to 3¼mm (No 10/US 3) needles. g with a k row, work in st st and patt m chart until Front measures same as ck to armhole shaping, ending with a ong side row. **
ape Armhole and Neck
st off 5 (6:7) sts at beg of next row. ork 1 row. *** Dec 1 st at armhole edge next 2 rows. Now dec 1 st at each end of t 6 (5:5) rows.
l and 3rd sizes only: Dec 1 st at nhole edge on next (3:5) rows, **at the ne time**, dec 1 st at neck edge on (1:2) right side rows.
sizes: [24 (27:29) sts.] Keeping nhole edge straight, dec 1 st at neck edge next 3 (1:1) rows, then on every alt row il 14 (16:18) sts rem. Cont straight until ont measures same as Back to shoulder ping, ending at armhole edge.
ape Shoulder
st off 7 (8:9) sts at beg of next row. ork 1 row. Cast off rem 7 (8:9) sts.

GHT FRONT
ork as given for Left Front to **. Work 1 v.
ape Armhole and Neck
st off 5 (6:7) sts at beg of next row. mplete as given for Left Front from ***.

Fair Isle Waistcoat

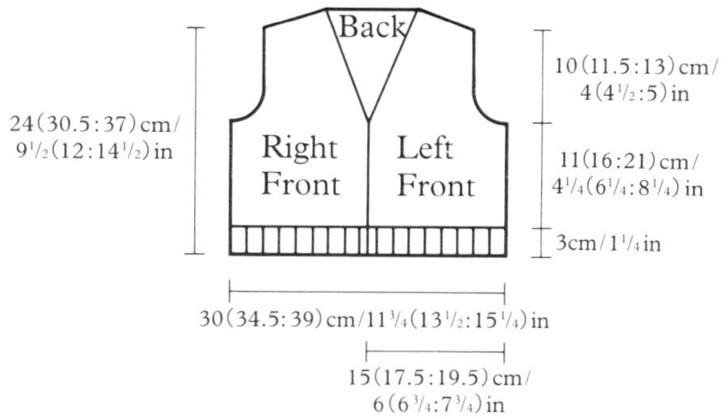

Back
Right Front
Left Front
24(30.5:37)cm/ 9½(12:14½)in
10(11.5:13)cm/ 4(4½:5)in
11(16:21)cm/ 4¼(6¼:8¼)in
3cm/1¼in
30(34.5:39)cm/11¾(13½:15¼)in
15(17.5:19.5)cm/ 6(6¾:7¾)in

FRONT BAND
Join shoulder seams.
With right side facing, using 2¾mm (No 12/US 2) needles and A, pick up and k42 (54:68) sts up straight edge of Right Front, k27 (31:35) sts along shaped edge to shoulder, k back neck sts, pick up and k27 (31:35) sts down shaped edge of Left Front to beg of neck shaping and k42 (54:68) sts down straight edge. [169 (203:241) sts.]
Beg with a 2nd row, work 2 rows in rib as given for Back welt.

Buttonhole row: Rib to last 42 (54:66) sts, [yrn, p2 tog, rib 10] 3 (4:5) times, yrn, p2 tog, rib 4.
Rib 2 rows. Cast off in rib.

ARMBANDS
With right side facing, using 2¾mm (No 12/US 2) needles and A, pick up and k67 (77:87) sts evenly around armhole edge.
Beg with a 2nd row, work 5 rows in rib as given for Back welt. Cast off in rib.

TO MAKE UP
Join side and armband seams. Sew on buttons.

triped Top with Sailor Collar page 26

ATERIALS
5:5) x 50g balls of Rowan Cotton ce in Green (A).
4:5) balls in White (B).
air each of 2¾mm (No 12/US 2) and mm (No 10/US 3) knitting needles.

EASUREMENTS

fit age	2	3	4	years
ual chest	71	76	82	cm
asurement	28	30	32¼	in
gth	40	43	46	cm
	15¾	17	18	in
eve seam	24	28	31	cm
	9½	11	12¼	in

NSION
sts and 34 rows to 10cm/4in square r st st on 3¼mm (No 10/US 3) dles.

BREVIATIONS
page 44.

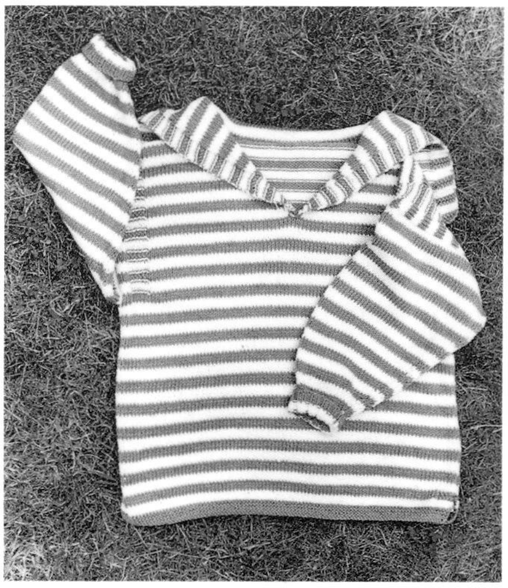

BACK
With 2¾mm (No 12/US 2) needles and A, cast on 92 (98:106) sts. K 7 rows.
Change to 3¼mm (No 10/US 3) needles.
1st row (right side): K.
2nd row: K5, p to last 5 sts, k5.
Rep last 2 rows once. Change to B and rep 1st and 2nd rows twice.
Beg with a k row, work in st st and stripe patt of 4 rows A and 4 rows B until Back measures 24 (25:26)cm/9½ (10:10¼)in from beg, ending with 4th row of A or B stripe.
Cont in stripe patt, work as follows:
Next row: K5, p6, k to last 11 sts, p6, k5.
Next row: P. **
Rep last 2 rows until Back measures 40 (43:46)cm/15¾ (17:18)in from beg, ending with a wrong side row.

Shape Shoulders
Cast off 24 (26:29) sts at beg of next 2 rows. Cast off rem 44 (46:48) sts.

FRONT
Work as given for Back to **. Rep last 2 rows until Front measures 29 (32:35)cm/ 11½ (12¾:13¾)in from beg, ending with a wrong side row.
Shape Neck
Next row: Patt 46 (49:53), turn.
Work on this set of sts only. Dec 1 st at neck edge on every row until 34 (35:37) sts rem, then on every foll alt row until 24 (26:29) sts rem. Cont straight until Front matches Back to shoulder shaping, ending at side edge. Cast off.
With right side facing, rejoin yarn to rem sts, patt to end. Complete as first side.

SLEEVES
With 2¾mm (No 12/US 2) needles and A, cast on 38 (42:46) sts.
1st row (right side): With A, k2, [p2, k2] to end.
2nd row: With A, p2, [k2, p2] to end.
Rep last 2 rows once more. Change to B and rep 1st and 2nd rows twice. Rep last 8 rows once more, inc 6 sts evenly across last row. [44 (48:52) sts.]
Change to 3¼mm (No 10/US 3) needles.
Beg with a k row, work in st st and stripe patt of 4 rows A and 4 rows B, **at the same time**, inc 1 st at each end of 3rd row and every foll 2nd row until there are 88 (70:62) sts, then on every foll 3rd row until there are 94 (100:106) sts. Cont straight until Sleeve measures 24 (28:31)cm/9½ (11:12¼)in from beg, ending with a wrong side row. Cast off.

COLLAR

With 2¾mm (No 12/US 2) needles and A, cast on 86 (92:98) sts. K 5 rows.
Change to 3¼mm (No 10/US 3) needles.
1st row (right side): With A, p6, k to last 6 sts, p6.
2nd row: With A, p.
Rep last 2 rows once more. Change to B and rep 1st and 2nd rows twice. Rep last 8 rows until Collar measures 14cm/5½in from beg, ending with a wrong side row.
Next row: Patt 33, cast off next 20 (26:32) sts, patt to end.
Cont on last set of sts only for left front collar. Patt 1 row. Cast off 3 sts at beg of next row and foll alt row. Dec 1 st at inside edge on every right side row until 2 sts rem. Work 2 tog and fasten off.
With wrong side facing, rejoin yarn at inside edge to rem sts for right front collar and patt 2 rows. Complete as given for left front collar.

INSET

With 3¼mm (No 10/US 3) needles and B, cast on 3 sts. K 1 row. Beg with a p row, work in st st and inc 1 st at each end of every row until there are 35 sts. K 3 rows. Cast off.

TO MAKE UP

Join shoulder seams. Sew on sleeves, placing centre of sleeves to shoulder seams. Beginning at top of borders at sides, join side and sleeve seams. Sew on collar. Sew in inset.

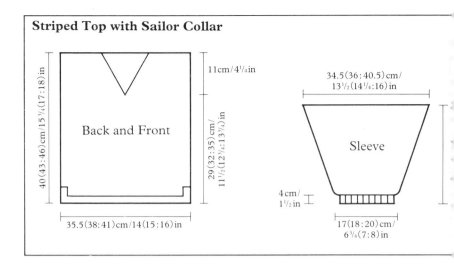

Striped Top with Sailor Collar

Back and Front
40(43:46)cm/15¾(17:18)in
35.5(38:41)cm/14(15:16)in
11cm/4¼in
29(32:35)cm/11½(12¼:13¾)in

Sleeve
34.5(36:40.5)cm/13½(14¼:16)in
4cm/1½in
17(18:20)cm/6¾(7:8)in

Zipped Fair Isle Jacket with Hat page 27

MATERIALS

Jacket: 5 (6) x 50g balls of Rowan Cotton Glace in Navy (A).
1 ball each in Green, Pink, Blue, Yellow and Violet.
1 pair each of 3mm (No 11/US 2) and 3¾mm (No 9/US 5) knitting needles.
1 of 30 (35)cm/12 (14)in long open-ended zip fastener.
Hat: 2 x 50g balls of Rowan Cotton Glace in Navy.
1 pair each of 3mm (No 11/US 2) and 3¾mm (No 9/US 5) knitting needles.

MEASUREMENTS

To fit age	1	2	years
Actual chest measurement	60	70	cm
	23½	27½	in
Length	35	40	cm
	13¾	15¾	in
Sleeve seam	20	24	cm
	8	9½	in

TENSION

25 sts and 29 rows to 10cm/4in square over pattern on 3¾mm (No 9/US 5) needles.

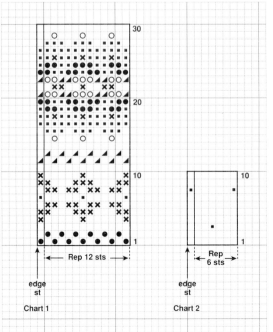

Rep 12 sts
edge st
Chart 1

Rep 6 sts
edge st
Chart 2

ABBREVIATIONS

See page 44.

NOTE

Read charts from right to left on right side (k) rows and from left to right on wrong side (p) rows. When working in pattern, strand yarn not in use loosely across wrong side to keep fabric elastic

KEY

☐	Navy (A)
●	Green
✖	Pink
▪	Blue
◣	Yellow
○	Violet

JACKET

BACK AND FRONTS
Worked in one piece to armholes.
With 3mm (No 11/US 2) needles and A, cast on 151 (175) sts.
1st row: K1, [p1, k1] to end.
This row forms moss st patt. Rep last row 7 times more.
Change to 3¾mm (No 9/US 5) needles.
Next row (right side): Moss st 3, k to last 3 sts, moss st 3.
Next row: Moss st 3, p to last 3 sts, moss st 3.
Using separate small ball of A yarn for each moss st front band and twisting yarns together on wrong side at joins, work border pattern as follows:
1st row: With A, moss st 3, k across 12 sts of 1st row of chart 1 to last 4 sts, k edge st, with A, moss st 3.
2nd row: With A, moss st 3, p edge st of 2nd row of chart 1, p across 12 sts to last 3 sts, with A, moss st 3.
Work a further 12 rows as set.
Work in main patt as follows:
1st row: With A, moss st 3, k 6 sts of 1st row of chart 2 to last 4 sts, k edge st, with A, moss st 3.
2nd row: With A, moss st 3, p edge st of 2nd row of chart 2, p across 6 sts to last 3 sts, with A, moss st 3.
Work a further 38 (48) rows as set.
Now work in yoke patt as given for border patt, work 2 rows.

Divide for Armholes
Next row: Patt 39 (45), turn.
Work on this set of sts only for Right Front.
** Keeping patt correct, work a further 25 (27) rows.

Shape Neck
Next row: Patt 5 (6) and slip these sts on to a safety pin, patt to end.
Patt 1 row. Cast off 3 (4) sts at beg of next row. Dec 1 st at neck edge on every row until 23 (26) sts rem. Patt 4 (3) rows.

Shape Shoulder
Cast off 11 (13) sts at beg of next row.
Work 1 row. Cast off rem 12 (13) sts.
With right side facing, rejoin yarn to rem sts, patt 73 (85), turn. Work on this set of sts only for Back. Patt 37 (41) rows.

Shape Shoulders
Cast off 11 (13) sts at beg of next 2 rows and 12 (13) sts at beg of foll 2 rows.
Leave rem 27 (33) sts on a holder.
With right side facing, rejoin yarn to rem sts for Left Front. Complete as given for Right Front from ** to end.

SLEEVES
With 3mm (No 11/US 2) needles and A, cast on 37 (41) sts.
1st row (right side): K1, [p1, k1] to end.
2nd row: P1, [k1, p1] to end.
Rep last 2 rows until cuff measures 3 (4)cm/1¼ (1½)in, ending with a 1st row.
Inc row: Rib 2 (3), m1, [rib 3 (5), m1] to last 2 (3) sts, rib 2 (3). [49 sts.]
Change to 3¾mm (No 9/US 5) needles.
Beg with a k row, work 2 rows in st st.
Work 1st to 14th rows of chart 1 for border patt, then work 20 (30) rows of main patt from chart 2, rep 1st to 14th rows of chart 1 again, **at the same time**, inc 1 st at each end of 3rd row and 8 (11) foll 5th (4th) rows, working inc sts into patt. [67 (73) sts.] Cast off.

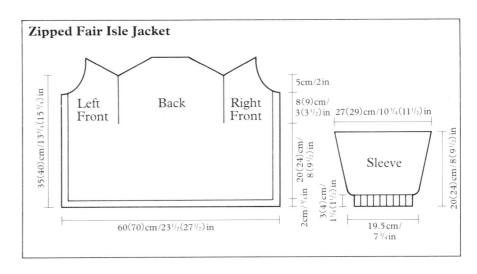

Zipped Fair Isle Jacket

COLLAR
Join shoulder seams.
With right side facing and using 3mm (No 11/US 2) needles, slip 5 (6) sts from Right Front safety pin on to needle, rejoin A yarn and pick up and k19 (20) sts up right front neck, work across back neck sts as follows: k3, [m1, k3] 8 (10) times, pick up and k19 (20) sts down left front neck, then k2 (3), moss st 3 sts from Left Front safety pin. [83 (95) sts.]
Work 1 row in moss st.
Next 2 rows: Moss st to last 24 sts, turn.
Next 2 rows: Moss st to last 21 sts, turn.
Cont in this way, working 3 sts more at end of next 10 rows, turn, moss st to end. Work 2 rows.
Next row: Moss st 2, inc in next st, m1, moss st to last 3 sts, m1, inc in next st, moss st 2.
Work 3 rows. Rep last 4 rows 4 times more. Cast off loosely in patt.

TO MAKE UP
Sew in sleeves, placing centre of sleeves to shoulder seams. Join sleeve seams.
Sew in zip.

HAT
With 3mm (No 11/US 2) needles, cast on 99 (111) sts.
1st row: K1, [p1, k1] to end.
This row forms moss st. Rep last row until work measures 4cm/1½in from beg.
Next row: P1, [k1, p1] to end.
Next row: K1, [p1, k1] to end.
Rep last 2 rows for 4cm/1½in.
Change to 3¾mm (No 9/US 5) needles.
Cont in moss st until work measures 14 (17)cm/5½ (6¾)in from beg.
Shape Top
Dec row: Moss st 3, [p3 tog, moss st 13 (15)] to end.
Moss st 7 rows.
Dec row: Moss st 3, [p3 tog, moss st 11 (13)] to end.
Moss st 7 rows.
Dec row: Moss st 3, [p3 tog, moss st 9 (11)] to end.
Moss st 5 rows.
Dec row: Moss st 3, [p3 tog, moss st 7 (9)] to end.
Moss st 5 rows. Cont in this way, dec 12 sts as set on next row and 2 (3) foll 4th rows. [15 sts.] Moss st 3 rows.
Dec row: Moss st 3, [p3 tog, moss st 3] twice.
Moss st 3 rows.
Dec row: Moss st 3, [p3 tog, moss st 1] twice.
Break off yarn, thread end through rem sts, pull up and secure. Join seam, reversing seam on brim. Turn back brim.

MATERIALS

4 x 100g hanks of Rowan Magpie Aran in Red (A).
1 hank each in Cream (B) and Maroon (C).
1 pair each of 4mm (No 8/US 6) and 5mm (No 6/US 8) knitting needles.
1 of 35cm/14in long open-ended zip fastener.
2 buttons.

MEASUREMENTS

To fit age	3-5	years
Actual chest measurement	88 34½	cm in
Length	41 16	cm in
Sleeve seam	24 9½	cm in

TENSION

17 sts and 25 rows to 10cm/4in square over st st on 5mm (No 6/US 8) needles.
20 sts and 19 rows to 10cm/4in square over pattern on 5mm (No 6/US 8) needles.

ABBREVIATIONS

See page 44.

NOTE

When working in pattern, strand yarn not in use loosely across wrong side to keep fabric elastic.

LEFT FRONT

With 4mm (No 8/US 6) needles and A, cast on 43 sts.
1st row: K1, [p1, k1] to end.
This row forms moss st. Rep last row 5 times more, inc 1 st at centre of last row. [44 sts.]
Change to 5mm (No 6/US 8) needles.

1st row (right side): K3A, [2B, 2A] to last 5 sts, 2B, with A, moss st 3.
2nd row: With A, moss st 3, Ayf, [p2B, 2A] to last st, p1A.
3rd row: K3C, [2A, 2C] to last 5 sts, 2A, with A, moss st 3.
4th row: With A, moss st 3, [p2A, 2C] to last st, p1C.
These 4 rows form patt. Cont in patt until Front measures 23cm/9in from beg, ending with a wrong side row.
Shape Armhole
Cast off 4 sts at beg of next row. [40 sts.]
Cont in patt until Front measures 36cm/14in from beg, ending with a wrong side row.
Shape Neck
Next row: Patt to last 5 sts, turn; leave the 5 sts on a safety pin.
Keeping patt correct, dec 1 st at neck edge on every row until 28 sts rem. Cont straight until Front measures 41cm/16in from beg, ending with a wrong side row.
Shape Shoulder
Cast off 14 sts at beg of next row. Work 1 row. Cast off rem 14 sts.

RIGHT FRONT

With 4mm (No 8/US 6) needles and A, cast on 43 sts. Work 6 rows in moss st as given for Left Front welt, inc 1 st at centre of last row. [44 sts.]
Change to 5mm (No 6/US 8) needles.
1st row (right side): With A, moss st 3, [k2B, 2A] to last st, k1A.
2nd row: P3A, [2B, 2A] to last 5 sts, 2B, with A, moss st 3.
3rd row: With A, moss st 3, [k2A, 2C] to last st, k1C.
4th row: P3C, [2A, 2C] to last 5 sts, 2A, with A, moss st 3.
These 4 rows form patt. Complete as given for Left Front, reversing shapings.

BACK

With 4mm (No 8/US 6) needles and A, cast on 75 sts. Work 6 rows in moss st as given for Left Front welt.
Change to 5mm (No 6/US 8) needles.
Beg with a k row, work in st st until Back measures same as Left Front to armhole shaping, ending with a p row.

Shape Armholes
Cast off 4 sts at beg of next 2 rows. [67 sts]
Cont straight until Back measures same a Left Front to shoulder shaping, ending wi a p row.
Shape Shoulders
Cast off 12 sts at beg of next 4 rows. Leav rem 19 sts on a holder.

SLEEVES

With 4mm (No 8/US 6) needles and A, cast on 29 sts. Work 5 rows in moss st as given for Left Front.
Inc row: Moss st 2, [m1, moss st 3] 9 times. [38 sts.]
Change to 5mm (No 6/US 8) needles.
Beg with a k row, work in st st, inc 1 st at each end of every 3rd row until there are (sts. Cont straight until Sleeve measures 26cm/10¼in from beg, ending with a p row. Cast off.

COLLAR

Join shoulder seams.
With right side facing, using 4mm (No 8/US 6) needles and A, slip 5 sts from Right Front safety pin on to needle, pick u and k18 sts up right front neck, work acro back neck sts as follows: k2, [m1, k2] 8 times, pick up and k18 sts down left front neck, then k2, moss st 3 sts from Left Fro safety pin. [73 sts] Work 1 row in moss st
Next 2 rows: Moss st to last 21 sts, turn.
Next 2 rows: Moss st to last 18 sts, turn.
Next 2 rows: Moss st to last 15 sts, turn.
Next 2 rows: Moss st to last 12 sts, turn.
Work to end, then work 20 rows in moss s across all sts. Cast off loosely in moss st.

STRAPS (make 2)

With 4mm (No 8/US 6) needles and A, cast on 21 sts. Work 6 rows in moss. Cast off in moss st.

TO MAKE UP

Sew on sleeves, placing centre of sleeves t shoulder seams and sewing ends of last 6 rows of sleeve tops to cast off sts at armholes. Place straps on top of front welt and sew short ends to side of welts. Join side and sleeve seams. Secure other ends c straps in position with buttons. Sew in zip

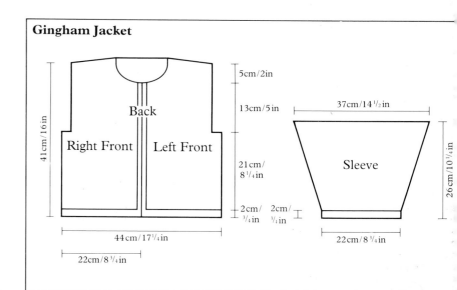

Gingham Jacket

Back

Right Front | Left Front

41cm/16in

44cm/17¼in

22cm/8¾in

5cm/2in

13cm/5in

21cm/8¼in

2cm/¾in   2cm/¼in

37cm/14½in

Sleeve

26cm/10¼in

22cm/8¾in

Cardigan with Lace Edging page 31

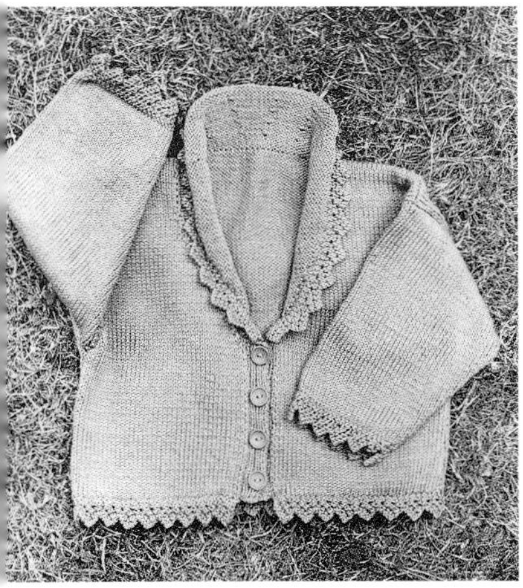

ATERIALS
(6:7) x 50g balls of Rowan Cotton
ace.
pair each of 2¾mm (No 12/US 2) and
¼mm (No 10/US 3) knitting needles.
buttons.

EASUREMENTS

fit age	1	2	3	years
ctual chest	65	70	76	cm
easurement	25½	27½	30	in
ngth	30	32	34	cm
	12	12¾	13½	in
eeve seam	21	23	26	cm
	8¼	9	10¼	in

ENSION
sts and 34 rows to 10cm/4in square
er st st on 3¼mm (No 10/US 3)
edles.

BBREVIATIONS
e page 44.

ACK
ith 3¼mm (No 10/US 3) needles, cast on
(92:99) sts.
ork in st st until Back measures 27
9:31)cm/10¾ (11½:12¼)in from beg,
ding with a p row.
ape Shoulders
ast off 8 (9:10) sts at beg of next 4 rows
d 8 sts at beg of foll 2 rows. Cast off rem
(40:43) sts.

EFT FRONT
ith 3¼mm (No 10/US 3) needles, cast on
(42:46) sts.
ork in st st until Front measures 13
4:15)cm/5¼ (5½:6)in from beg, ending
th a p row.
ape Neck
ec 1 st at end of next row and at same
ge on every foll 3rd row until 24 (26:28)
s rem. Cont straight for a few rows until
ont measures same as Back to shoulder
aping, ending with a p row.
ape Shoulder
ast off 8 (9:10) sts at beg of next row and
l alt row. Work 1 row. Cast off rem 8 sts.

RIGHT FRONT
Work as given for Left Front, reversing shapings.

SLEEVES
With 3¼mm (No 10/US 3) needles, cast on 52 (60:66) sts. Work in st st, inc 1 st at each end of 3rd row and every foll 4th (5th:6th) row until there are 78 (84:90) sts. Cont straight until Sleeve measures 18 (20:23)cm/7 (8:9)in from beg, ending with a p row. Cast off.

COLLAR
Join shoulder seams.
With wrong side facing and using 2¾mm (No 12/US 2) needles, pick up and k33 (36:39) sts up left front neck, 30 (32:34) sts across back neck and 33 (36:39) sts down right front neck. [96 (104:112) sts.] Beg with a k row, work 6 rows in reverse st st, dec 1 st at each end of every alt row.
Next row: K32 (35:38), m1, [k6 (6:7), m1] twice, k2 (4:2), m1, [k6 (6:7), m1] twice, k to end.
Work 3 rows, dec 1 st at each end of 1st and 3rd rows. [92 (100:108) sts.]
Next row: K2 tog, k28 (31:34), m1, [k7 (7:8), m1] twice, k4 (6:4), m1, [k7 (7:8), m1] twice, k28 (31:34), k2 tog.
Work 3 rows, dec 1 st at each end of every row. [90 (98:106) sts.]
Next row: K2 tog, k24 (27:30), m1, [k8 (8:9), m1] twice, k6 (8:6), m1, [k8 (8:9), m1] twice, k24 (27:30), k2 tog.
Work 3 rows, dec 1 st at each end of every row. [88 (96:104) sts.]
Next row: K22 (25:28), m1, [k9 (9:10), m1] twice, k8 (10:8), m1, [k9 (9:10), m1] twice, k 22 (25:28).
Cast off 3 sts at beg of next 4 rows. Cast off rem 82 (90:98) sts.

BUTTON BAND
With 2¾mm (No 12/US 2) needles, cast on 8 sts. Work in p1, k1 rib until band, when slightly stretched, fits along front edge of Left Front. Cast off in rib.
Sew in place. Mark band to indicate position of 4 buttons: first one 2cm/¾in up from lower edge, last one 1cm/¼in below top and rem 2 evenly spaced between.

BUTTONHOLE BAND
With 2¾mm (No 12/US 2) needles, cast on 8 sts. Work in k1, p1 rib and complete as given for Button Band, making buttonholes at markers as follows:
1st buttonhole row (right side): Rib 3, cast off 2, rib to end.
2nd buttonhole row: Rib 3, cast on 2, rib to end.

COLLAR EDGING
With 2¾mm (No 12/US 2) needles, cast on 4 sts. K 1 row.
1st row (right side): K2, yf, k2.
2nd row and 2 foll alt rows: Sl 1, k to end.
3rd row: K3, yf, k2.
5th row: K2, yf, k2 tog, yf, k2.
7th row: K3, yf, k2 tog, yf, k2.
8th row: Cast off 4, k to end.
These 8 rows form patt. Cont in patt until edging, when slightly stretched, fits around outside edge of collar, ending with 8th patt row. Cast off.

CUFF EDGINGS
Work as given for Collar Edging until edging, when slightly stretched, fits along lower edge of Sleeve, ending with 8th patt row. Cast off.

WELT EDGING
Work as given for Collar Edging until edging, when slightly stretched, fits along lower edge of Back and Fronts, ending with 8th patt row. Cast off.

TO MAKE UP
Sew on cuff edgings. Placing centre of sleeves to shoulder seams, sew on sleeves. Join side and sleeve seams. Sew on collar and welt edgings. Join short edges of collar edging to front bands. Sew on buttons.

Cardigan with Lace Edging

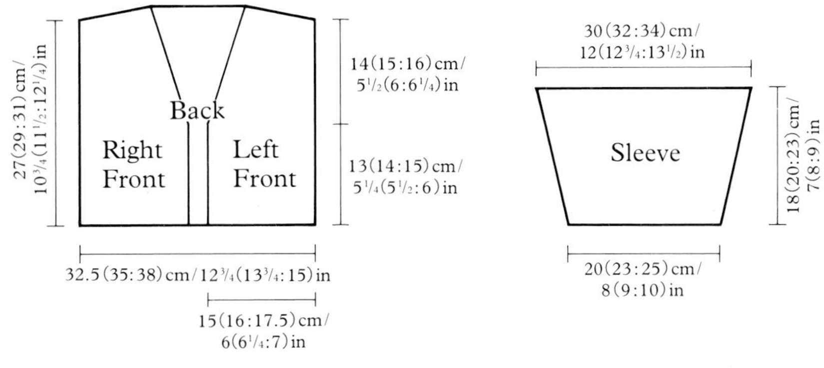
27(29:31)cm/
10¾(11½:12¼)in
Back
Right Front
Left Front
14(15:16)cm/
5½(6:6¼)in
13(14:15)cm/
5¼(5½:6)in
32.5(35:38)cm/12¾(13¾:15)in
15(16:17.5)cm/
6(6¼:7)in
30(32:34)cm/
12(12¾:13½)in
Sleeve
18(20:23)cm/
7(8:9)in
20(23:25)cm/
8(9:10)in

Cable and Bobble Aran Sweater page 32

MATERIALS

8 x 100g hanks of Rowan Magpie Aran.
1 pair each of 4mm (No 8/US 6) and
5mm (No 6/US 8) knitting needles.
Cable needle.

MEASUREMENTS

To fit age	5–6	years
Actual chest measurement	102 40	cm in
Length	46 18	cm in
Sleeve seam	30 12	cm in

TENSION

26 sts and 26 rows to 10cm/4in square
over pattern on 5mm (No 6/US 8)
needles.

ABBREVIATIONS

Cr3L = sl next 2 sts on to cable needle
and leave at front of work, p1, then k2
from cable needle;
Cr3R = sl next st on to cable needle and
leave at back of work, k2, then p1 from
cable needle.
Also see page 44.

PANEL A

Worked over 14 sts.
1st row (wrong side): P2, k3, p4, k3, p2.
2nd row: K2, p3, sl next 2 sts on to cable
needle and leave at back of work, k2, then
k2 from cable needle, p3, k2.
3rd row: As 1st row.
4th row: K2, p2, Cr3R, Cr3L, p2, k2.
5th row: P2, [k2, p2] 3 times.
6th row: K2, p1, Cr3R, p2, Cr3L, p1, k2.
7th row: P2, k1, p2, k4, p2, k1, p2.
8th row: K2, p1, k2, p4, k2, p1, k2.
9th row: As 7th row.
10th row: K2, p1, Cr3L, p2, Cr3R, p1, k2.
11th row: As 5th row.
12th row: K2, p2, Cr3L, Cr3R, p2, k2.
These 12 rows form patt.

PANEL B

Worked over 19 sts.
1st row (wrong side): K4, k into front,
back, front, back and front of next st, k2,
p2, k1, p2, k2, k into front, back, front,
back and front of next st, k4.
2nd row: P4, k5 tog tbl, p2, sl next 3 sts on
to cable needle and leave at front of work,
k2, sl first st on cable needle back on to left
hand needle, p this st, then k2 from cable
needle, p2, k5 tog tbl, p4.
3rd row: K7, p2, k1, p2, k7.
4th row: P6, Cr3R, p1, Cr3L, p6.
5th row: K6, p2, k3, p2, k6.
6th row: P5, Cr3R, p3, Cr3L, p5.
7th row: K5, p2, k2, k into front, back,
front, back and front of next st, k2, p2, k5.
8th row: P4, Cr3R, p2, k5 tog tbl, p2,
Cr3L, p4.
9th row: K4, p2, k7, p2, k4.
10th row: P3, Cr3R, p7, Cr3L, p3.
11th row: K3, p2, k2, k into front, back,
front, back and front of next st, k3, k into
front, back, front, back and front of next st,
k2, p2, k3.
12th row: P2, Cr3R, p2, k5 tog tbl, p3, k5
tog tbl, p2, Cr3L, p2.
13th row: K2, p2, k11, p2, k2.
14th row: P2, k2, p11, k2, p2.
15th row: K2, p2, k3, [k into front, back,
front, back and front of next st, k3] twice,
p2, k2.
16th row: P2, Cr3L, p2, k5 tog tbl, p3, k5
tog tbl, p2, Cr3R, p2.
17th row: K3, p2, k9, p2, k3.
18th row: P3, Cr3L, p7, Cr3R, p3.
19th row: K4, p2, k3, k into front, back,
front, back and front of next st, k3, p2, k4.

20th row: P4, Cr3L, p2, k5 tog tbl, p2,
Cr3R, p4.
21st row: K5, [p2, k5] twice.
22nd row: P5, Cr3L, p3, Cr3R, p5.
23rd row: As 5th row.
24th row: P6, Cr3L, p1, Cr3R, p6.
These 24 rows form patt.

BACK

With 4mm (No 8/US 6) needles, cast on
130 sts.
1st row: P2, [k2, p2] to end.
2nd row: K2, [p2, k2] to end.
Rep last 2 rows 4 times more.
Inc row: Rib 33, [m1, rib 32] twice, m1,
rib 33. [133 sts.]
Change to 5mm (No 6/US 5) needles.
1st row (wrong side): K1, ★ [k1, p1, k1]
all in next st, p3 tog ★; rep from ★ to ★ onc
k1, work 1st row of panel A, [work 1st ro
of panel B, then 1st row of panel A] 3
times, k1, rep from ★ to ★ twice, k1.
2nd row: P10, work 2nd row of panel A,
[work 2nd row of panel B, then 2nd row c
panel A] 3 times, p10.
3rd row: K1, ★ p3 tog, [k1, p1, k1] all in
next st ★; rep from ★ to ★ once, k1, work
3rd row of panel A, [work 3rd row of pane
B, then 3rd row of panel A] 3 times, k1, r
from ★ to ★ twice, k1.
4th row: P10, work 4th row of panel A,
[work 4th row of panel B, then 4th row of
panel A] 3 times, p10.
These 4 rows form patt for side edges and
set position of panels. Cont in patt until
Back measures approximately 46cm/18in
from beg, ending with 13th row of panel I
Shape Shoulders
Cast off 22 sts at beg of next 4 rows. Leav
rem 45 sts on a holder.

FRONT

Work as given for Back until Front
measures approximately 41cm/16in from
beg, ending with 1st row of panel B.
Shape Neck
Next row: Patt 53, work 2 tog, turn.
Work on this set of sts only. Keeping patt
correct, dec 1 st at neck edge on every row
until 44 sts rem. Patt 1 row.
Shape Shoulder
Cast off 22 sts at beg of next row. Work 1
row. Cast off rem 22 sts.

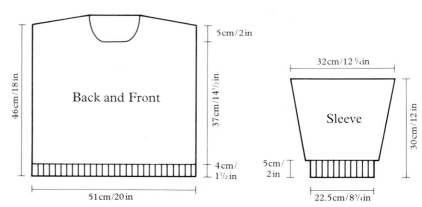

Cable and Bobble Aran Sweater

Back and Front
46cm/18in
37cm/14½in
5cm/2in
4cm/1½in
51cm/20in

Sleeve
32cm/12¾in
30cm/12in
5cm/2in
22.5cm/8¾in

...th right side facing, sl centre 23 sts on to
...older, rejoin yarn to rem sts, work 2 tog,
...t to end. Dec 1 st at neck edge on every
...w until 44 sts rem. Patt 2 rows.
...ape Shoulder
...st off 22 sts at beg of next row. Work 1
...v. Cast off rem 22 sts.

...EEVES
...th 4mm (No 8/US 6) needles, cast on 38
... Beg with a 2nd row, work 14 rows in
... as given for Back welt.
... row: Rib 2, m1, rib 1, m1, rib 3, m1,
...1, m1, rib 4, m1, rib 1, m1, rib 3, [m1,
...1] 8 times, m1, rib 3, m1, rib 1, m1, rib
...m1, rib 1, m1, rib 3, m1, rib 1, m1, rib
...[59 sts.]
...ange to 5mm (No 6/US 8) needles.
... row (wrong side): K1, [k1, p1, k1] all
...next st, p3 tog, k1, work 1st row of panel
...1st row of panel B, then 1st row of panel
...k1, [k1, p1, k1] all in next st, p3 tog, k1.
...d row: P6, work 2nd row of panel A,
...d row of panel B, then 2nd row of panel
...p6.
...i row: K1, p3 tog, [k1, p1, k1] all in
...xt st, k1, work 3rd row of panel A, 3rd
...w of panel B, then 3rd row of panel A,
...p3 tog, [k1, p1, k1] all in next st, k1.
... row: P6, work 4th row of panel A, 4th
...w of panel B, then 4th row of panel A,

...ese 4 rows form patt for side edges and
... position of panels. Cont in patt, inc 1 st
...each end of next row and every foll 4th
...w until there are 83 sts, working inc sts
...o side edge patt. Cont straight until
...eve measures 30cm/12in from beg,
...ding with a wrong side row. Cast off.

...ECKBAND
...n right shoulder seam.
...th right side facing and using 4mm (No
...JS 6) needles, pick up and k16 sts down
... front neck, work across centre front sts
...follows: k2, p2, k2 tog, k1, p2, k2, p
...ce in next st, k2, p2, k1, k2 tog, p2, k2,
...k up and k15 sts up right front neck,
...rk across back neck sts as follows: k1,
..., k2] 3 times, p2 tog, p1, k2, p2, k2, p
...ce in next st, k2, p2, k2, p1, k2 tog, p1, [k2,
...] 3 times, k twice in last st. [98 sts.] Beg
...h a 1st row, work 12 rows in rib as given
... Back welt. Change to 5mm (No 6/US
...needles. Rib 15 rows. Cast off in rib.

...) MAKE UP
...n left shoulder and neckband seam,
...ersing seam on last 8cm/3in of
...ckband. Sew on sleeves, placing centre of
...eves to shoulder seams. Join side and
...eve seams.

Patterned Coat page 33

MATERIALS

5 (6) x 100g hanks of Rowan Magpie
Aran in Navy (A).
1 hank each in Green, Gold, Red, Cream
and Turquoise.
1 pair each of 4mm (No 8/US 6) and
5mm (No 6/US 8) knitting needles.
1 each of 4mm (No 8/US 6) and 5mm
(No 6/US 8) circular knitting needles.
7 (8) buttons.

MEASUREMENTS

To fit age	3–4	5–6	years
Actual chest measurement	83 32¾	93 36½	cm in
Length	47 18½	53 21	cm in
Sleeve seam	26 10¼	30 12	cm in

TENSION

18 sts and 22 rows to 10cm/4in square
over pattern on 5mm (No 6/US 8)
needles.

ABBREVIATIONS

See page 44.

NOTE

Read chart from right to left on right side
(k) rows and from left to right on wrong
side (p) rows. When working in Fair Isle
pattern, strand yarn not in use loosely
across wrong side over no more than 5
sts to keep fabric elastic.

POCKET LININGS (make 2)

With 5mm (No 6/US 8) needles and A,
cast on 19 sts. Beg with a k row, work 32
rows in st st. Leave these sts on a holder.

BACK AND FRONTS

Worked in one piece to armholes.
With 4mm (No 8/US 6) circular needle and
A, cast on 151 (169) sts. Work forwards
and backwards in rows.
1st row: K1, [p1, k1] to end.
This row forms moss st. Rep this row 9
times more, inc 4 sts evenly across last row.
[155 (173) sts.]
Change to 5mm (No 6/US 8) circular
needle.
Next row (right side): Moss st 5, k to last
5 sts, moss st 5.
Next row: Moss st 5, p to last 5 sts, moss
st 5.
Using separate small balls of A yarn for
each moss st front band and twisting yarns
together on wrong side at joins, work in
patt as follows:
1st row: With A, moss st 5, k across 18 sts
of 1st row of chart 8 (9) times, k edge st,
with A, moss st 5.
2nd row: With A, moss st 5, p edge st of
2nd row of chart, then p across 18 sts 8 (9)
times, with A, moss st 5.
These 2 rows set patt. Work a further 4
rows as set.
Buttonhole row: Patt 2, k2 tog, yf, patt to
end.
Patt 11 rows, then rep the buttonhole row.
Patt 8 rows.
Place Pockets
Next row: Patt 10, with A, p1, [k1, p1] 9
times, patt to last 29 sts, with A, p1, [k1,
p1] 9 times, patt 10.
Rep last row once more.
Next row: Patt 10, with A, cast off in moss
st next 19 sts, patt to last 29 sts, with A,
cast off in moss st next 19 sts, patt to end.
Next row: Patt 2, k2 tog, yf, patt 6, patt
across sts of first pocket lining, patt to last
10 sts, patt across sts of second pocket
lining, patt to end.
Patt a further 25 (33) rows, making
buttonholes as before on every 12th row.

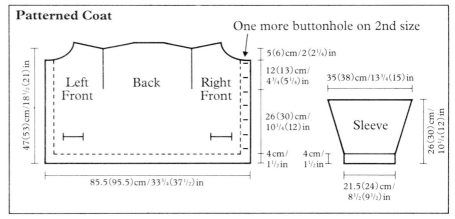

Patterned Coat

One more buttonhole on 2nd size

47(53)cm/18½(21)in

Left Front — Back — Right Front

5(6)cm/2(2¼)in
12(13)cm/4¾(5¼)in
26(30)cm/10¼(12)in
4cm/1½in — 4cm/1½in
35(38)cm/13¾(15)in

85.5(95.5)cm/33¾(37½)in

Sleeve
26(30)cm/10¼(12)in
21.5(24)cm/8½(9½)in

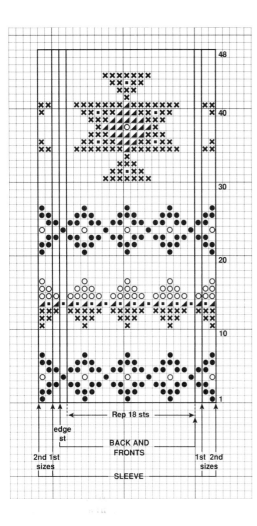

Rep 18 sts

edge
st

BACK AND
FRONTS

2nd 1st
sizes

1st 2nd
sizes

SLEEVE

Star Sweater page

MATERIALS
5 (6) x 50g balls of Rowan Cotton Gla·
in Navy (A).
1 ball each in Lilac, Green, Red,
Turquoise and Gold.
1 pair each of 2¾mm (No 12/US 2) an
3¼mm (No 10/US 3) knitting needles.
1 button.

MEASUREMENTS

To fit age	12–18	18–24	month
Actual chest measurement	70 27½	76 30	cm in
Length	31 12¼	36 14¼	cm in
Sleeve seam	19 7½	24 9½	cm in

TENSION
26 sts and 34 rows to 10cm/4in square
over st st on 3¼mm (No 10/US 3)
needles.

ABBREVIATIONS
See page 44.

NOTE
Read charts from right to left on right
side (k) rows and from left to right on
wrong side (p) rows. When working
border pattern, strand yarn not in use
loosely across wrong side to keep fabric
elastic. Use separate lengths of contras·
colours when working in main pattern,
twisting yarns together on wrong side a
joins to avoid holes.

Divide for Armholes
Next row: Patt 40 (45), inc in next st,
turn.
Work on this set of 42 (47) sts only for
Right Front. Keeping patt correct, work a
further 25 (27) rows making buttonholes
on 10th (2nd) row and 1 (2) foll 12th rows.
Shape Neck
Next row: Cast off 3, patt 5 sts more and
slip these 6 sts on to a safety pin, patt to
end.
Dec 1 st at neck edge on every row until 26
(28) sts rem. Patt 5 (4) rows.
Shape Shoulder
Cast off 13 (14) sts at beg of next row. Patt
1 row. Cast off rem 13 (14) sts.
With right side facing, rejoin yarn to rem
sts, patt 73 (81), turn. Work on this set of
sts only for Back. Patt 37 (41) rows.
Shape Shoulders
Cast off 13 (14) sts at beg of next 4 rows.
Leave rem 21 (25) sts on a holder.
With right side facing, rejoin yarn to rem
sts for Left Front, inc in first st, patt to end.
Complete as given for Right Front,
omitting buttonholes and reversing
shapings.

SLEEVES
With 4mm (No 8/US 6) needles and A,
cast on 31 (35) sts. Work 10 rows in moss
st as given for Back and Fronts welt.
Inc row: Moss st 1 (3), [m1, moss st 4]
7 times, m1, moss st 2 (4). [39 (43) sts.]
Change to 5mm (No 6/US 8) needles.
P 1 row. K 1 row. Cont in st st and patt
from chart, inc 1 st at each end of next row
and every foll 4th row until there are 63
(69) sts, working inc sts into patt. Patt 3 (7)
rows straight. Cast off.

COLLAR
Join shoulder seams.
With right side facing and using 4mm (No
8/US 6) needles, slip 6 sts from Right Front
safety pin on to needle, join A yarn and
pick up and k16 (18) sts up right front
neck, work across back sts as follows: k3
(1), [m1, k3] 6 (8) times, pick up and k16
(18) sts down left front neck, then k5, p1
sts from Left Front safety pin. [71 (81) sts.]
Next row: P1, [k1, p1] to end.
This row forms moss st.
Next 2 rows: Moss st to last 22 (24) sts,
turn.
Next 2 rows: Moss st to last 19 (21) sts,
turn.
Cont in this way, working 3 sts more at end
of next 6 (8) rows, turn and work to end.
Work 26 rows in moss st across all sts. Cast
off loosely in patt.

TO MAKE UP
Sew in sleeves, placing centre of sleeves to
shoulder seams. Join sleeve seams. Catch
down pocket linings. Sew on buttons.

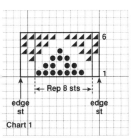

Chart 1

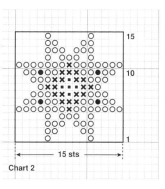

Chart 2

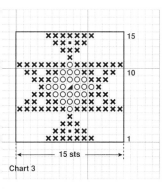

Chart 3

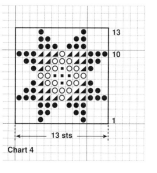

Chart 4

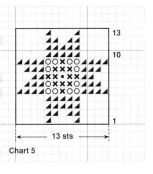

Chart 5

KEY

- ☐ Navy
- ☐ Lilac
- ☐ Green
- ◑ Red
- ☒ Turquoise
- ☐ Gold

BACK

With 2¾mm (No 12/US 2) needles and A, cast on 91 (99) sts.

1st row (right side): K1, [p1, k1] to end.

2nd row: P1, [k1, p1] to end.

Rep last 2 rows until welt measures 3cm/1¼in, ending with a wrong side row. Change to 3¼mm (No 10/US 3) needles. Beg with a k row, work in st st and border patt from chart 1 for 6 rows.

Work in main patt as follows: with A, work 4 (6) rows in st st.

Next row: K6 (7)A, * k across 1st row of chart 2, k6 (8)A, k across 1st row of chart 3 *; k7 (9)A, rep from * to *, k6 (7)A.

Next row: P6 (7)A, * p across 2nd row of chart 3, p6 (8)A, p across 2nd row of chart 2 *; p7 (9)A, rep from * to *, p6 (7)A.

Work a further 13 rows as set. With A, work 7 (11) rows in st st.

Next row: K1A, [k across 1st row of chart 4, k6 (8)A, k across 1st row of chart 5, k6 (8)A] twice, k across 1st row of chart 4, k1A.

Next row: P1A, [p across 2nd row of chart 4, p6 (8)A, p across 2nd row of chart 5, p6 (8)A] twice, p across 2nd row of chart 4, p1A.

Work a further 11 rows as set. With A, work 7 (11) rows in st st.

Next row: K6 (7)A, * k across 1st row of chart 3, k6 (8)A, k across 1st row of chart 2 *; k7 (9)A, rep from * to *, k6 (7)A.

Next row: P6 (7)A, *p across 2nd row of chart 2, p6 (8)A, p across 2nd row of chart 3 *; p7 (9)A, rep from * to *, p6 (7)A.

Work a further 13 rows as set. ** With A, work 5 (9) rows in st st.

Divide for Opening

Next row: With A, k44 (48), k2 tog, turn. Work on this set of sts only.

Next row: With A, k3, p to end.

Next row: K1A, k across 1st row of chart 5, k6 (8)A, k across 1st row of chart 4, k12 (14)A.

Next row: With A, k3, p9 (11), p across 2nd row of chart 4, p6 (8)A, p across 2nd row of chart 5, p1A.

Work a further 11 rows as set. Keeping the 3 sts at inside edge in garter st (every row k), cont in A only, work 1 (5) rows.

Shape Shoulder

Cast off 11 (12) sts at beg of next row and foll alt row and 12 sts at beg of foll alt row. Leave rem 11 (13) sts on a holder.

With right side facing, rejoin A yarn to rem sts, k to end.

Next row: P to last 3 sts, k3.

Next row: K12 (14)A, k across 1st row of chart 4, k6 (8)A, k across 1st row of chart 5, k1A.

Next row: P1A, p across 2nd row of chart 5, p6 (8)A, p across 2nd row of chart 4, with A, p9 (11), k3.

Work a further 11 rows as set. Keeping the 3 sts at inside edge in garter st, cont in A only, work 2 (6) rows. Complete as given for first side.

FRONT

Work as given for Back to **. With A, work 7 (11) rows in st st.

Next row: K1A, k across 1st row of chart 5, k6 (8)A, k across 1st row of chart 4, k25 (29)A, k across 1 st row of chart 4, k6 (8)A, k across 1st row of chart 5, k1A.

Next row: P1A, p across 2nd row of chart 5, p6 (8)A, p across 2nd row of chart 4, p25 (29)A, p across 2nd row of chart 4, p6 (8)A, p across 2nd row of chart 5, p1A.

Shape Neck

Next row: Patt 38 (41), turn.

Work on this set of sts only. Keeping patt correct, dec 1 st at neck edge on next 4 (5) rows. [34 (36) sts.] Patt 6 (5) rows. Cont in A only, work 1 (5) rows.

Shape Shoulder

Cast off 11 (12) sts at beg of next row and foll alt row. Work 1 row. Cast off rem sts.

With right side facing, slip centre 15 (17) sts on to a holder, rejoin yarn to rem sts, patt to end. Dec 1 st at neck edge on next 4 (5) rows. [34 (36) sts.] Patt 6 (5) rows. Cont in A only, work 2 (6) rows. Complete as given for first side.

SLEEVES

With 2¾mm (No 12/US 2) needles and A, cast on 37 (41) sts. Work 3 (4)cm/1¼ (1½)in in rib as given for Back welt, ending with a right side row.

Inc row: Rib 4 (3), m1, [rib 6 (4), m1] to last 3 (2) sts, rib 3 (2). [43 (51) sts.]

Change to 3¼mm (No 10/US 3) needles. Beg with a k row, work in st st and border patt from chart 1 for 6 rows, inc 1 st at each end of 5th row. [45 (53) sts.]

Work in main patt as follows: with A, work 4 (6) rows in st st, inc 1 st at each end of 2nd (3rd) row. [47 (55) sts.]

Next row: With A, k twice in first st, k4 (7), k across 1st row of chart 3, k7 (9)A, k across 1st row of chart 2, with A, k4 (7), k twice in last st.

Next row: P6 (9)A, p across 2nd row of chart 2, p7 (9)A, p across 2nd row of chart 3, p6 (9)A.

Work a further 13 rows as set, inc 1 st at each end of 2nd (3rd) row and 3 (2) foll 3rd (4th) rows, working inc sts in A. [57 (63) sts.] With A, work 7 (11) rows, inc 1 st at each end of 1st (2nd) row and 2 foll 3rd (4th) rows. [63 (69) sts.]

Next row: K6 (7)A, k across 1st row of chart 5, k6 (8)A, k across 1st row of chart 4, k6 (8)A, k across 1st row of chart 5, k6 (7)A.

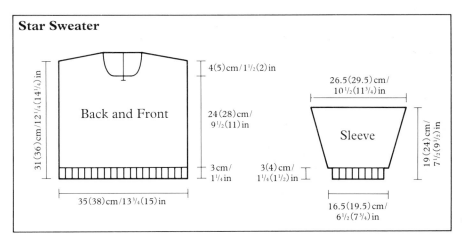

Star Sweater

Back and Front — 31 (36)cm/12¼(14¼)in; 24 (28)cm/9½(11)in; 4(5)cm/1½(2)in; 3cm/1¼in; 35(38)cm/13¾(15)in

Sleeve — 26.5(29.5)cm/10½(11¾)in; 19(24)cm/7½(9½)in; 3(4)cm/1¼(1½)in; 16.5(19.5)cm/6½(7¾)in

Next row: P6 (7)A, p across 2nd row of chart 5, p6 (8)A, p across 2nd row of chart 4, p6 (8)A, p across 2nd row of chart 5, p6 (7)A.

Work a further 11 rows as set, inc 1 st at each end of next row and 2 foll 3rd (4th) rows. [69 (75) sts.] With A, work 7 (13) rows in st st, inc 1 st at each end of 2nd row on **2nd size** only. [69 (77) sts.] Cast off.

COLLAR

Join shoulder seams.

With right side facing and using 2¾mm (No 12/US 2) needles and A, k sts from left back neck, pick up and k19 (22) sts down left front neck, k centre front sts, pick up and k19 (22) sts up right front neck, then k sts from right back neck. [75 (87) sts.]

Next row: K4, [p1, k1] to last 3 sts, k3.
Next row: K3, [p1, k1] to last 4 sts, p1, k3.
Rep last 2 rows twice more.
Next row: K3, rib 31 (37), k2, k2 tog, turn.
Work on this set of sts only.
Next row: K3, rib to last 3 sts, k3.
Rep last row 14 (16) times more. K 3 rows. Cast off.
Rejoin yarn at centre front to rem sts.
Next row: K3, rib to last 3 sts, k3.
Rep last row 15 (17) times more. K 3 rows. Cast off.

TO MAKE UP

Sew on sleeves, placing centre of sleeves to shoulder seams. Join side and sleeve seams. Make buttonhole loop at base of collar on left back neck. Sew button to other side.

Aran Cardigan with Tie Collar

MATERIALS

8 (8:9) x 50g balls of Rowan Cotton Glace.
1 pair each of 3¼mm (No 10/US 3) and 3¾mm (No 9/US 5) knitting needles.
1 of 3¼mm (No 10/US 3) circular knitting needle.
Cable needle.
4 buttons.

MEASUREMENTS

To fit age	1	2	3	years
Actual chest measurement	67	70	73	cm
	26½	27½	28¾	in
Length	31	33	35	cm
	12¼	13	13¾	in
Sleeve seam	21	23	26	cm
	8¼	9	10¼	in

TENSION

26 sts and 36 rows to 10cm/4in square over moss stitch on 3¾mm (No 9/US 5) needles.

ABBREVIATIONS

Cr3L = sl next 2 sts on to cable needle and leave at front of work, p1, then k2 from cable needle;
Cr3R = sl next st on to cable needle and leave at back of work, k2, then p1 from cable needle;
C4 = sl next 2 sts on to cable needle and leave at front of work, k2, then k2 from cable needle;
mb = [k1, p1] twice in next st, turn, p4, turn, sl 2, k2 tog, pass 2 slipped sts over. Also see page 44.

PANEL A

Worked over 6 sts.
1st row (right side): P1, mb, p1, Cr3R.
2nd row: K1, p2, k3.
3rd row: P2, Cr3R, p1.
4th row: K2, p2, k2.
5th row: P1, Cr3R, p2.
6th row: K3, p2, k1.
7th row: Cr3R, p3.
8th row: K4, p2.
9th row: Cr3L, p1, mb, p1.
10th row: K3, p2, k1.
11th row: P1, Cr3L, p2.
12th row: K2, p2, k2.
13th row: P2, Cr3L, p1.
14th row: K1, p2, k3.
15th row: P3, Cr3L.
16th row: P2, k4.
These 16 rows form patt.

PANEL B

Worked over 11 sts.
1st row (right side): P2, Cr3R, k1, Cr3L, p2.
2nd row: K2, p2, k1, p1, k1, p2, k2.
3rd row: P1, Cr3R, k1, p1, k1, Cr3L, p1.
4th row: K1, p2, k1, [p1, k1] twice, p2, k1.
5th row: Cr3R, k1, [p1, k1] twice, Cr3L.
6th row: P2, k1, [p1, k1] 3 times, p2.
7th row: K3, [p1, k1] 3 times, k2.
8th row: P3, [k1, p1] 3 times, p2.
9th row: Cr3L, k1, [p1, k1] twice, Cr3R.
10th row: K1, p3, [k1, p1] twice, p2, k1.
11th row: P1, Cr3L, k1, p1, k1, Cr3R, p1.
12th row: K2, p3, k1, p3, k2.
13th row: P2, Cr3L, k1, Cr3R, p2.
14th row: K3, p5, k3.
15th row: P3, sl next 3 sts on to cable needle and leave at back of work, k2, then p1, k2 sts from cable needle, p3.
16th row: K3, p2, k1, p2, k3.
These 16 rows form patt.

BACK

With 3¼mm (No 10/US 3) needles, cast on 93 (97:101) sts.
1st row: K1, [p1, k1] to end.
This row forms moss st. Rep last row 8 times more.
Inc row: Moss st 10 (12:14), [m1, moss st 6] 13 times, moss st to end. [106 (110:114) sts.]
Change to 3¾mm (No 9/US 5) needles.
1st row (right side): Moss st 9 (11:13), p1, k4, p1, work 1st row of panel A, p1, k4, p1, work 1st row of panel B, p1, k4, p1, work 1st row of Panel A, p1, k4, p1, work 9th row of Panel A, p1, k4, p1, work 1st row of panel B, p1, k4, p1, work 9th row of panel A, p1, k4, p1, moss st 9 (11:13).
2nd row: Moss st 9 (11:13), k1, p4, k1, work 10th row of panel A, k1, p4, k1, work 2nd row of panel B, k1, p4, k1, work 10th row of panel A, k1, p4, k1, work 2nd row of panel A, k1, p4, k1, work 2nd row of panel B, k1, p4, k1, work 2nd row of panel A, k1, p4, k1, moss st 9 (11:13).
3rd row: Moss st 9 (11:13), p1, C4, p1, work 3rd row of panel A, p1, C4, p1, work 3rd row of panel B, p1, C4, p1, work 3rd row of panel A, p1, C4, p1, work 11th row of panel A, p1, C4, p1, work 3rd row of panel B, p1, C4, p1, work 11th row of panel A, p1, C4, p1, moss st 9 (11:13).
4th row: Moss st 9 (11:13), k1, p4, k1, work 12th row of panel A, k1, p4, k1, work 4th row of panel B, k1, p4, k1, work 12th row of panel A, k1, p4, k1, work 4th row of panel

k1, p4, k1, work 4th row of panel A, k1,
k1, moss st 9 (11:13).
ese 4 rows form cable patt and set
sition of panels. Cont in patt until Back
asures 31 (33:35)cm/12¼ (13:13¾)in
m beg, ending with a wrong side row.

ape Shoulders

st off 11 (11:12) sts at beg of next 4 rows
d 11 (12:11) sts at beg of foll 2 rows.
ave rem 40 (42:44) sts on a holder.

FT FRONT

th 3¼mm (No 10/US 3) needles, cast on
(51:53) sts. Work 9 rows in moss st as
en for Back welt.
c row: Moss st 8, [m1, moss st 6] 6
es, moss st to end. [55 (57:59) sts.]
ange to 3¾mm (No 9/US 5) needles.
row (right side): Moss st 9 (11:13),
k4, p1, work 1st row of panel A, p1, k4,
work 1st row of panel B, p1, k4, p1,
rk 1st row of panel A, moss st 5.
d row: Moss st 5, work 2nd row of panel
k1, p4, k1, work 2nd row of panel B, k1,
k1, work 2nd row of panel A, k1, p4,
moss st 9 (11:13).
d row: Moss st 9 (11:13), p1, C4, p1,
rk 3rd row of panel A, p1, C4, p1, work
d row of panel B, p1, C4, p1, work 3rd
w of panel A, moss st 5.
row: Moss st 5, work 4th row of panel
k1, p4, k1, work 4th row of panel B, k1,
k1, work 4th row of panel A, k1, p4, k1,
ss st 9 (11:13).
ese 4 rows form cable patt and set
sition of panels. Cont in patt until Front
asures 16 (17:18)cm/6¼ (6¾:7)in from
g, ending with a wrong side row.

ape Neck

xt row: Patt to last 8 sts, turn; leave the
ts on a safety pin.
eping patt correct, dec 1 st at neck edge
9 foll right side rows, then on every foll
d row until 33 (34:35) sts rem. Cont
aight until Front measures same as Back
shoulder shaping, ending at side edge.

ape Shoulder

st off 11 (11:12) sts at beg of next row
d foll alt row. Work 1 row. Cast off rem
(12:11) sts.
ark straight front edge to indicated
sition of 4 buttons: first one 4 rows up
m cast on edge, last one 2 rows down
m beg of neck shaping and rem 2 evenly
aced between.

RIGHT FRONT

With 3¼mm (No 10/US 3) needles, cast on
49 (51:53) sts. Work 4 rows in moss st as
given for Back welt.
Buttonhole row (right side): K1, p1, k2
tog, yf, patt to end.
Work 4 rows.
Inc row: Moss st 11 (13:15), [m1, k6] 6
times, moss st 2. [55 (57:59) sts.]
Change to 3¾mm (No 9/US 5) needles.
1st row (right side): Moss st 5, work 9th
row of panel A, p1, k4, p1, work 1st row of
panel B, p1, k4, p1, work 9th row of panel
A, p1, k4, p1, moss st 9 (11:13).
2nd row: Moss st 9 (11:13), k1, p4, k1,
work 10th row of panel A, k1, p4, k1, work
2nd row of panel B, k1, p4, k1, work 10th
row of panel A, moss st 5.
3rd row: Moss st 5, work 11th row of
panel A, p1, C4, p1, work 3rd row of panel
B, p1, C4, p1, work 11th row of panel A,
p1, C4, p1, moss st 9 (11:13).
4th row: Moss st 9 (11:13), k1, p4, k1,
work 12th row of panel A, k1, p4, k1, work
4th row of panel B, k1, p4, k1, work 12th
row of panel A, moss st 5.
These 4 rows form cable patt and set
position of panels. Cont in patt until Front
measures 16 (17:18)cm/6¼ (6¾:7)in from
beg, ending with a right side row, **at the
same time,** making buttonholes as before
to match markers on Left Front. Complete
as given for Left Front.

SLEEVES

With 3¼mm (No 10/US 3) needles, cast on
45 (49:53) sts. Work 9 rows in moss st as
given for Back welt.
Inc row: Moss st 6 (8:4), m1, [moss st 3
(3:4), m1] 11 times, moss st 6 (8:5). [57
(61:65) sts.]
Change to 3¾mm (No 9/US 5) needles.
1st row (right side): Moss st 5 (7:9), p1,
k4, p1, work 1st row of panel A, p1, k4, p1,
work 1st row of panel B, p1, k4, p1, work
9th row of panel A, p1, k4, p1, moss st 5
(7:9).
2nd row: Moss st 5 (7:9), k1, p4, k1, work
10th row of panel A, k1, p4, k1, work 2nd
row of panel B, k1, p4, k1, work 2nd row of
panel A, k1, p4, k1, moss st 5 (7:9).
3rd row: Moss st 5 (7:9), p1, C4, p1, work
3rd row of panel A, p1, C4, p1, work 3rd
row of panel B, p1, C4, p1, work 11th row
of panel A, p1, C4, p1, moss st 5 (7:9).
4th row: Moss st 5 (7:9), k1, p4, k1, work
12th row of panel A, k1, p4, k1, work 4th
row of panel B, k1, p4, k1, work 4th row of
panel A, k1, p4, k1, moss st 5 (7:9).
These 4 rows form cable patt and set
position of panels. Cont in patt, inc 1 st at
each end of next row and every foll 5th

(5th:6th) row until there are 75 (81:87) sts,
working inc sts into moss st. Cont straight
until Sleeve measures 21 (23:26)cm/8¼
(9:10¼)in from beg, ending with a wrong
side row. Cast off.

COLLAR

Join shoulder seams.
With right side facing and using 3¼mm
(No 10/US 3) needles, slip sts from Right
Front safety pin on to needle, pick up and
k43 (46:49) sts up shaped edge to shoulder,
work across back neck sts as follows: k2
(3:4), [m1, k3] 12 times, m1, k2 (3:4), pick
up and k43 (46:49) sts down shaped edge
of Left Front to beg of neck shaping, k3,
moss st 5 across sts from safety pin. [155
(163:171) sts.] Work 1 row in moss st.
Next 2 rows: Moss st to last 48 (51:54) sts,
turn.
Next 2 rows: Moss st to last 45 (48:51) sts,
turn.
Next 2 rows: Moss st to last 42 (45:48) sts,
turn.
Cont in this way, working 3 sts more at end
of next 20 (22:24) rows, turn, moss st to
end. Cast off 6 sts at beg of next 2 rows.
Change to 3¼mm (No 10/US 3) circular
needle and work forwards and backwards
as follows:
Cast on 86 sts at beg of next 2 rows. [315
(323:331) sts.] Dec 1 st at each end of next
15 rows. Cast off in moss st.

TO MAKE UP

Sew on sleeves, placing centre of sleeves to
shoulder seams. Join side and sleeve seams.
Sew on buttons.

Aran Cardigan with Tie Collar

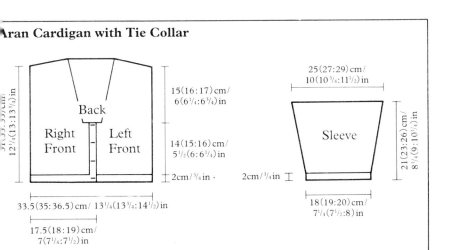

Back

Right Front   Left Front

15(16:17)cm/
6(6¼:6¾)in

14(15:16)cm/
5½(6:6¼)in

2cm/¾in

31(33:35)cm/
12¼(13:13¾)in

33.5(35:36.5)cm/ 13¼(13¾:14½)in

17.5(18:19)cm/
7(7¼:7½)in

25(27:29)cm/
10(10¾:11½)in

Sleeve

21(23:26)cm/
8¼(9:10¼)in

2cm/¾in

18(19:20)cm/
7¼(7½:8)in

Tartan All-in-one with Beret page 36

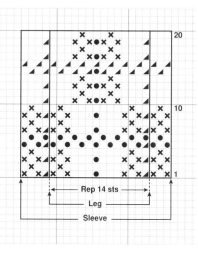

MATERIALS

All-in-one: 4 x 50g balls of Rowan Designer DK Wool in Red (A).
2 balls in Navy (B).
1 ball each in Green and Yellow.
1 pair each of 3¼mm (No 10/US 3) and 4mm (No 8/US 6) knitting needles.
1 of 25cm/10in long zip fastener.
Beret: 2 x 50g balls of Rowan Designer DK Wool.
1 pair each of 3¼mm (No 10/US 3) and 4mm (No 8/US 6) knitting needles.

MEASUREMENTS

To fit age	3-6	months
Actual chest measurement	58 22¾	cm in
Length	49 19¼	cm in
Sleeve seam	17 6¾	cm in
Inside leg seam	15 6	cm in

TENSION

24 sts and 28 rows to 10cm/4in square over pattern on 4mm (No 8/US 6) needles.

ABBREVIATIONS

See page 44.

NOTE

Read chart from right to left on right side (k) rows and from left to right on wrong side (p) rows. When working in pattern, use separate small balls of yarn for each coloured area and twist yarns together on wrong side at joins to avoid holes.

ALL-IN-ONE

LEFT LEG

With 3¼mm (No 10/US 3) needles and B, cast on 48 sts. Work 11 rows in k1, p1 rib.
Inc row: Rib 7, [m1, rib 5] to last st, rib 1. [56 sts.]
Change to 4mm (No 8/US 6) needles.
Beg with a k row, work in st st and patt from chart, inc 1 st at each end of 3rd row and every foll alt row until there are 82 sts, working inc sts into patt. Patt 7 rows.
Shape Crotch
Cast off 3 sts at beg of next 2 rows.
Keeping patt correct, dec 1 st at each end of next row and 2 foll alt rows. [70 sts.]
Patt 1 row. ** Leave sts on a spare needle.

RIGHT LEG

Work as given for Left Leg to **.

MAIN PART

Next row: Patt across sts of Right Leg then Left Leg, working twice in last st. [141 sts.]
Patt 7 rows.
Next row: With A, k4, patt to last 4 sts, with A, k4.
Rep last row until work measures 35cm/13¾in from beg, ending with a right side row.
Divide for Armholes
Next row: K4A, patt 31, cast off 1 st, patt to last 36 sts, cast off 1 st, patt to last 4 sts, k4A.
Next row: K4A, patt 31, turn.
Work on this set of sts only for Right Front for a further 10cm/4in, ending with a wrong side row.
Shape Neck
Next row: K4A, patt 4 and slip these 8 sts on to a safety pin, patt to end.
Dec 1 st at neck edge on every row until 22 sts rem. Cont straight until work measures 49cm/19¼in from beg, ending with a right side row.
Shape Shoulder
Cast off 11 sts at beg of next row. Work 1 row. Cast off rem 11 sts.
With right side facing, rejoin yarn to rem sts, patt 69, turn. Cont on this set of sts only for Back until work measures 49cm/19¼in from beg, ending with a wrong side row.

KEY

☐	Red (A)
✖	Navy (B)
◢	Green
●	Yellow

Shape Shoulders
Cast off 11 sts at beg of next 4 rows. Leav rem 25 sts on a holder.
With right side facing, rejoin yarn to rem sts for Left Front, patt to last 4 sts, k4A. Complete to match Right Front, reversin shapings.

SLEEVES

With 3¼mm (No 10/US 3) needles and cast on 40 sts. Work 11 rows in k1, p1 rib.
Inc row: Rib 4, [m1, rib 4] to end. [49 sts.]
Change to 4mm (No 8/US 6) needles.
Beg with a k row, work in st st and patt from chart, inc 1 st at each end of every 3 row until there are 69 sts, working inc sts into patt. Cont straight until Sleeve measures 17cm/6¾in from beg, ending with a wrong side row. Cast off.

COLLAR

Join shoulder seams.
With right side facing, using 3¼mm (No 10/US 3) needles and B, slip 8 sts fro Right Front safety pin on to needle, pick

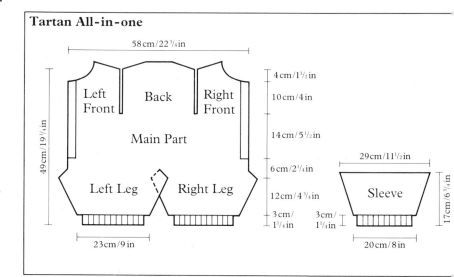

Tartan All-in-one

Left Front — Back — Right Front

Main Part

Left Leg — Right Leg

58cm/22¾in

49cm/19¼in

4cm/1½in
10cm/4in
14cm/5½in
6cm/2¼in
12cm/4¾in
3cm/1¼in

23cm/9in

Sleeve

29cm/11½in
3cm/1¼in
17cm/6¾in
20cm/8in

d k18 sts up right front neck, k across
ck neck sts, pick up and k18 sts down left
nt front neck, then k sts from safety pin. [77
.] K 3 rows.
c row: K4, [m1, k7] 10 times, m1, k3.
 sts.]
 rows.
c row: K4, [m1, k8] 10 times, m1, k4.
 sts.]
 rows.
Next row: K9, turn.
ork on these 9 sts only.
xt row: K2 tog, k to last 2 sts, k2 tog
.
 1 row. Rep last 2 rows twice.
xt row: Sl 1, k2 tog, psso and fasten off.
ith right side facing, rejoin yarn to rem
, rep from * until all sts are worked off.

TO MAKE UP

Join legs and crotch seams, then centre
front seam to beginning of garter st
borders. Sew in sleeves, placing centre of
sleeves to shoulder seams. Join sleeve
seams. Sew in zip.

BERET

With 3¼mm (No 10/US 3) needles, cast on
73 sts. K 9 rows.
Change to 4mm (No 8/US 6) needles.
Inc row: K1, [m1, k3] to end. [97 sts.]
K 3 rows.
Inc row: K1, [m1, k6] to end. [113 sts.]
K 3 rows.
Inc row: K1, [m1, k7] to end. [129 sts.]
K 3 rows.

Inc row: K1, [m1, k8] to end. [145 sts.]
Cont in this way, inc 16 sts as set on 3 foll
4th rows. [193 sts.]
K 14 rows.
Dec row: [K10, k2 tog] to last st, k1.
K 3 rows.
Dec row: [K9, k2 tog] to last st, k1.
K 3 rows.
Dec row: [K8, k2 tog] to last st, k1.
Cont in this way, dec 16 sts as set on every
foll 4th row until 33 sts rem. K 1 row.
Dec row: [K2 tog] to last st, k1.
Break off yarn, thread end through rem sts,
pull up and secure. Join seam.

3right Fair Isle Cardigan with Beret page 37

ATERIALS

ardigan: 4 (5:5) x 25g hanks of Rowan
ghtweight DK in Red (A).
 (3:4) hanks in Light Pink (B).
 (2:2) hanks in Turquoise.
 (2:2) hanks in Green.
 (1:1) hank each in Yellow and Dark
nk.
 pair each of 2¾mm (No 12/US 2) and
 4mm (No 10/US 3) knitting needles.
 buttons.

 eret: 2 x 25g hanks of Rowan
 ghtweight DK each in Red (A) and
 ght Pink (B).
 hank each in Turquoise (C), Green
 ), Yellow (E) and Dark Pink (F).
 pair each of 2¾mm (No 12/US 2) and
 4mm (No 10/US 3) knitting needles.

EASUREMENTS

fit age	6	9	12	months
ctual chest	61	69	77	cm
easurement	24	27	30¼	in
ngth	25	28	32	cm
	10	11	12½	in
eeve seam	17	19	23	cm
	6¾	7½	9	in

ENSION

 sts and 34 rows to 10cm/4in square
 er pattern on 3¼mm (No 10/US 3)
 edles.

BBREVIATIONS

e page 44.

OTE

ad chart from right to left on right side
) rows and from left to right on wrong
 de (p) rows. When working in pattern,
 and yarn not in use loosely across
 rong side to keep fabric elastic.

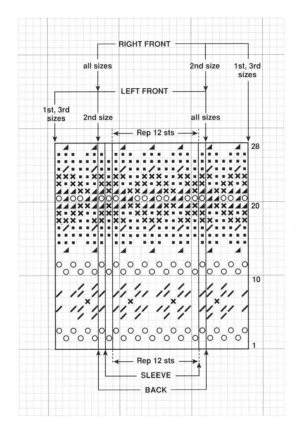

KEY

☐ Red (A)
■ Light Pink (B)
✕ Turquoise (C)
╱ Green (D)
○ Yellow (E)
◢ Dark Pink (F)

CARDIGAN

BACK

With 2¾mm (No 12/US 2) needles and A,
cast on 79 (89:99) sts.
1st row (right side): K1, [p1, k1] to end.
2nd row: P1, [k1, p1] to end.
Change to B and rib 5 rows.
Inc row: Rib 7 (8:5), inc in next st, [rib 8
(7:7), inc in next st] to last 8 (8:5) sts, rib 8
(8:5). [87 (99:111) sts.]
Change to 3¼mm (No 10/US 3) needles.
Beg with a k row, work in st st and patt
from chart until Back measures 25
(28:32)cm/10 (11:12½)in from beg, ending
with a wrong side row.

Shape Shoulders

Cast off 12 (14:16) sts at beg of next 2 rows
and 13 (15:17) sts at beg of foll 2 rows.
Leave rem 37 (41:45) sts on a holder.

LEFT FRONT

With 2¾mm (No 12/US 2) needles and A,
cast on 39 (45:49) sts. Work 2 rows in rib

as given for Back welt. Change to B and rib
5 rows.
Inc row: Rib 4 (4:3), inc in next st, [rib 5
(6:5), inc in next st] to last 4 (5:3) sts, rib 4
(5:3). [45 (51:57) sts.]
Change to 3¼mm (No 10/US 3) needles.
Beg with a k row, work in st st and patt
from chart until Front measures 21
(23:26)cm/8¼ (9:10¼)in from beg, ending
with right side row.

Shape Neck

Keeping patt correct, cast off 7 sts at beg of
next row and 4 sts at beg of foll alt row.
Dec 1 st at neck edge on every row until 25
(29:33) sts rem. Cont straight for a few
rows until Front matches Back to shoulder
shaping, ending with a wrong side row.

Shape Shoulder

Cast off 12 (14:16) sts at beg of next row.
Work 1 row. Cast off rem 13 (15:17) sts.

RIGHT FRONT

Work as given for Left Front, reversing shapings.

SLEEVES

With 2¾mm (No 12/US 2) needles and A, cast on 49 (51:53) sts. Work 2 rows in rib as given for Back welt. Change to B and rib 9 rows.

Inc row: Rib 2 (3:5), inc in next st, [rib 3 (4:5), inc in next st] to last 2 (2:5) sts, rib 2 (2:5). [61 sts.]

Change to 3¼mm (No 10/US 3) needles. Beg with a k row, work in st st and patt from chart until, inc 1 st at each end of every 3rd row until there are 83 (89:95) sts, working inc sts into patt. Cont straight until Sleeve measures 17 (19:23)cm/6¾ (7½:9)in from beg, ending with a wrong side row.
Cast off.

NECKBAND

Join shoulder seams.

With right side facing, using 2¾mm (No 12/US 2) needles and B, pick up and k25 (29:33) sts up left front neck, k back neck sts while dec 4 sts evenly, pick up and k25 (29:33) sts down left front neck. [83 (95:107) sts.] Beg with a 2nd row, work 6 rows in rib as given for Back welt. Change to A and rib 2 rows. Cast off in rib.

BUTTONHOLE BAND

With right side facing, using 2¾mm (No 12/US 2) needles and B, pick up and k63 (69:75) sts along front edge of Right Front, omitting first and last 2 rows of ribbed edgings. Beg with a 1st row, work 2 rows in rib as given for Back welt.

1st buttonhole row: Rib 2 (2:3), work 2 tog, yrn twice, work 2 tog, [rib 7 (8:9), work 2 tog, yrn twice, work 2 tog] 5 times, rib 2 (3:3).

2nd buttonhole row: Rib to end, working twice into 'yrn twice' of previous row.
Rib 2 rows. Change to A and rib 2 rows. Cast off in rib.

With right side facing, using 2¾mm (No 12/US 2) needles and A, pick up and k7 sts across one row end edge of band. Work 2nd then 1st rows of rib as given for Back welt. Cast off in rib. Work other end in same way.

BUTTON BAND

Work to match Buttonhole Band, omitting buttonholes.

TO MAKE UP

Sew on sleeves, placing centre of sleeves to shoulder seams. Join side and sleeve seams. Join front band edgings to main part. Sew on buttons.

BERET

With 2¾mm (No 12/US 2) needles and A, cast on 104 sts. Work 2 rows in k1, p1 rib. Change to B and rib 7 rows.

Inc row: Rib 2, [m1, rib 2, m1, rib 3] 20 times, m1, rib 2. [145 sts.]
Change to 3¼mm (No 10/US 3) needles. Beg with a k row, work in st st and patt from chart as indicated for Sleeve, work 1st to 3rd rows.

Inc row: With A, [p6, m1] to last st, p1. [169 sts.]
Work 5th to 9th rows of chart.

Inc row: With A, [p7, m1] to last st, p1. [193 sts.]
Work 11th and 12th rows of chart.

Inc row: With A, k1, [m1, k8] to end. [217 sts.]
Work 14th to 28th rows, then 1st to 3rd rows of chart.

Dec row: With A, [p7, p2 tog tbl] to last st, p1. [193 sts.]
Work 5th to 9th rows of chart.

Dec row: With A, [p6, p2 tog tbl] to last st, p1. [169 sts.]
Work 11th and 12th rows of chart.

Dec row: With A, k1, [skpo, k5] to end. [145 sts.]
Work 14th and 15th rows of chart.

Dec row: With B, p2 tog tbl, p9, [p3 tog tbl, p9] to last 2 sts, p2 tog tbl. [121 sts.]

Next row: K1B, * 1D, [3B, 1D] twice, 1B; rep from * to end.

Next row: P1B, [1C, 2B, 3C, 2B, 1C, 1B] to end.

Next row: K1C, [2B, 2C, 1B, 2C, 2B, 1C] to end.

Next row: P1C, [1F, 2C, 3F, 2C, 1F, 1C] to end.

Dec row: K1E, [2F, 1E, with F, k3 tog, 1E, 2F, 1E) to end. [97 sts.]

Next row: P1C, * 1F, [2C, 1F] twice, 1C; rep from * to end.

Next row: K1C, [2B, 1C, 1B, 1C, 2B, 1C] to end.

Next row: P1B, * 1C, [2B, 1C] twice, 1B; rep from * to end.

Next row: K1B, *1D, [2B, 1D] twice, 1B; rep from * to end.

Dec row: With B, p2, [p2 tog, p1, p2 tog, p3] to last 7 sts, [p2 tog, p1] twice, p1. [73 sts.]

Next row: K1A, [1B, 1A] to end.

Next row: P1A, [1F, 1A] to end.

Dec row: With A, k1, [k2 tog, k1] to end. [49 sts.]

Next row: P1A, [1E, 1A] to end.

Next row: K1E, [1A, 1E] to end.

Dec row: With A, p1, [p2 tog, p1] to end. [33 sts.]

Dec row: With A, k1, [k2 tog] to end. [17 sts.]

Dec row: With A, p1, [p2 tog] to end. [9 sts.]

Break off yarn, thread end through rem sts, pull up and secure. Join seam.

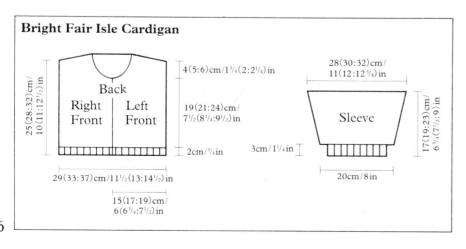

Bright Fair Isle Cardigan

Back Right Front Left Front

25(28:32)cm/ 10(11:12½)in

2cm/¾in

29(33:37)cm/11½(13:14½)in

15(17:19)cm/ 6(6¾:7½)in

4(5:6)cm/1¼(2:2¼)in

19(21:24)cm/ 7½(8¼:9½)in

28(30:32)cm/ 11(12:12¾)in

Sleeve

3cm/1¼in

20cm/8in

17(19:23)cm/ 6¾(7½:9)in

MATERIALS

Jacket: 3 x 50g balls of Rowan Cotton Glace in Cream (A).
2 balls in Light Blue (B).
1 ball each in Dark Blue (C), Light Green, Red, Dark Green and Pink.
1 pair of 3¼mm (No 10/US 3) knitting needles.
Crochet hook.
5 buttons.

Sandals: 1 x 50g ball of Rowan Cotton Glace in Light Blue (A).
Small amount of same in Dark Blue (B) and Cream (C).
1 pair of 3mm (No 11/US 2) knitting needles.
Crochet hook.
2 buttons.

MEASUREMENTS

To fit age	12–18	months
Actual chest measurement	64	cm
	25¼	in
Length	28	cm
	11	in
Sleeve seam	16	cm
	6¼	in

TENSION

27 sts and 30 rows to 10cm/4in square over check pattern on 3¼mm (No 10/US 3) needles.

ABBREVIATIONS

dc = double crochet. Also see page 44.

NOTE

Read charts from right to left on right side (k) rows and from left to right on wrong side (p) rows. When working check pattern, strand yarn not in use loosely across wrong side to keep fabric elastic. Use separate lengths of yarn for each coloured area when working flower motifs, twisting yarns together on wrong side at joins to avoid holes.

JACKET

BACK AND FRONTS

Worked in one piece to armholes.
With 3¼mm (No 10/US 3) needles and A, cast on 169 sts.
Beg with a k row, work in st st and patt from chart 1 until 7th row of chart has been worked. With A, p 1 row, inc 3 sts evenly across. [172 sts.]
Work in check patt as follows:
1st row (right side): K3B, [2C, 2B] to last st, 1B.
2nd row: P3B, [2C, 2B] to last st, 1B.
3rd row: K3A, [2B, 2A] to last st, 1A.
4th row: P3A, [2B, 2A] to last st, 1A.
These 4 rows form check patt. Work a further 14 rows in check patt.
Now work 24 rows of chart 2.

Divide for Armholes

Next row: With A, k42, k twice in next st, turn.
Work on this set of 44 sts only for Right Front. With A, p 1 row. Work in check patt, dec 1 st at beg of first row and every foll alt row until 29 sts rem. Cont straight until Front measures 27cm/10¾in from beg, ending with a right side row.

Shape Shoulder

Cast off 10 sts at beg of next row and foll alt row. Patt 1 row. Cast off rem 9 sts.
With right side facing, rejoin A yarn to rem sts, k twice in first st, k84, k twice in next st, turn. [88 sts.] Work on this set of sts only for Back. With A, p 1 row. Work in check patt until Back measures same as Right Front to shoulder shaping, ending with a wrong side row.

Shape Shoulders

Cast off 10 sts at beg of next 4 rows and 9 sts at beg of foll 2 rows. Cast off rem 30 sts.
With right side facing, rejoin A yarn to rem sts for Left Front, k twice in first st, k to end. Complete as given for Right Front, reversing shapings.

SLEEVES

With 3¼mm (No 10/US 3) needles and A, cast on 49 sts.
Beg with a k row, work in st st and patt from chart 1 until 7th row of chart has been worked.
Next row: With A, p twice in first st, [p23, p twice in next st] twice. [52 sts.]
Now work in check patt as given for Back and Fronts, inc 1 st at each end of 5 foll 3rd rows then on every foll 4th row until there are 68 sts, working inc sts into patt. Cont straight until Sleeve measures 15cm/6in from beg, ending with a wrong side row. Cast off.

TO MAKE UP

Join shoulder seams. Sew in sleeves, placing centre of sleeves to shoulder seams. Join sleeve seams. With right side facing, using crochet hook, A and beg at cast on edge of right front, work 1 row of dc up front edge, across back neck and down left front. Fasten off.
With right side facing, using crochet hook, B and beg at centre of back, work dc along lower edge of back and right front, 3 dc in corner, [1 dc in next dc] up straight front edge of right front making 5 buttonholes by working 2 chains and missing 2 dc, [1 dc in next dc] to shoulder, across back neck and down left front edge to lower edge, 3 dc in corner, work dc along lower edge of front to centre back, slip stitch in first dc. Do not turn. Work 1 row of backwards dc (dc worked from left to right). Fasten off.
With right side facing, using crochet hook and B, work 1 round of dc then 1 row of backwards dc along lower edge of sleeves. Fasten off. Sew on buttons.

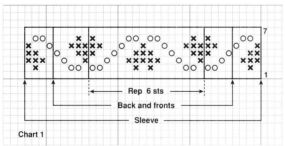

Rep 6 sts
Back and fronts
Sleeve
Chart 1

KEY

☐	Cream (A)
O	Light Green
✕	Red
◢	Dark Green
●	Pink

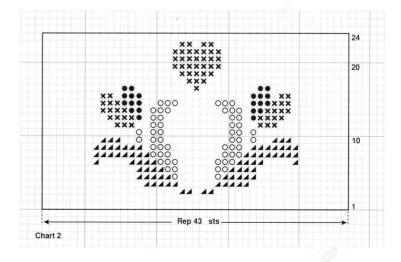

Rep 43 sts
Chart 2

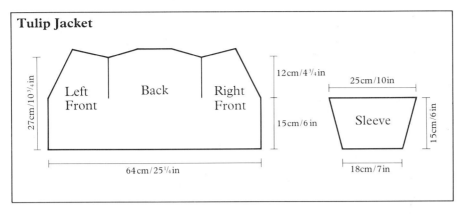

Tulip Jacket

Left Front | Back | Right Front

27cm/10¾in

64cm/25¼in

12cm/4¾in

15cm/6in

Sleeve

25cm/10in

15cm/6in

18cm/7in

SANDALS

LEFT SANDAL

With 3mm (No 11/US 2) needles and A, cast on 36 sts. K 1 row.
1st row (wrong side): K1, yf, k16, [yf, k1] twice, yf, k16, yf, k1.
2nd row and 4 foll alt rows: K to end but working k tbl into yf of previous row.
3rd row: K2, yf, k16, yf, k3, yf, k2, yf, k16, yf, k2.
5th row: K3, yf, k16, [yf, k4] twice, yf, k16, yf, k3.
7th row: K4, yf, k16, yf, k6, yf, k5, yf, k16, yf, k4.
9th row: K5, yf, k16, [yf, k7] twice, yf, k16, yf, k5.
11th row: K22, yf, k9, yf, k8, yf, k22. [64 sts.]

12th row: As 2nd row.
K 9 rows.
Shape Instep
Next row: K36, k2 tog, turn.
Next row: Sl 1, [p2B, 2A] twice, with A, p2 tog, turn.
Next row: Sl 1, [k2 A, 2B] twice, with A, k2 tog, turn.
Next row: Sl 1, [p2A, 2C] twice, with A, p2 tog, turn.
Next row: Sl 1, [k2C, 2A] twice, with A, k2 tog, turn.
Rep last 4 rows 3 times more.
Next row: Sl 1, [p2B, 2A] twice, with A, p2 tog, turn.
Next row: Sl 1, [k2 A, 2B] twice, with A, k to end.
Cont in A only.

Next row: K17, k2 tog, p8, k2 tog, k17. [44 sts.]
Next row: K24, turn.
Next row: P4, turn.
Next row: K4, turn.
Work in st st on these 4 sts only for 6cm/2¼in for front strap. Cast off.
With right side facing, rejoin A yarn at ba of strap, pick up and k12 sts along side edge of strap, turn and cast off knitwise a sts at this side of strap.
With right side facing, rejoin A yarn at top of other side of strap, pick up and k12 sts along side edge of strap then k rem 20 sts. Cast off knitwise.
Join sole and back seam.
With right side facing, using 3mm (No 11/US 2) needles, A and beg and ending within 9 sts of back seam, pick up and k1 sts along back heel for ankle strap. ★★
Next row: Cast on 4 sts, k to end, turn a cast on 22 sts. [44 sts.]
K 3 rows. Cast off knitwise.
With crochet hook, make buttonhole loop at long end of ankle strap, sew button to other end. Fold front strap over ankle stra to wrong side and slip stitch cast off edge.

RIGHT SANDAL
Work as given for Left Sandal to ★★.
Next row: Cast on 22 sts, k to end, turn and cast on 4 sts. [44 sts.]
Complete as given for Left Sandal.

Brilliant White Shirt page 41

MATERIALS
8 (9:10:11) x 50g balls of Rowan Cotton Glace.
1 pair each of 2¾mm (No 12/US 2) and 3¼mm (No 10/US 3) knitting needles.
Crochet hook.
7 buttons.

MEASUREMENTS

To fit age	3	4	5	6	years
Actual chest	79	84	90	94	cm
measurement	31	33	35½	37	in
Length	46	50	54	58	cm
	18	19¾	21¼	22¾	in
Sleeve seam	28	31	34	37	cm
	11	12¼	13½	14½	in

TENSION
26 sts and 34 rows to 10cm/4in square over st st on 3¼mm (No 10/US 3) needles.

ABBREVIATIONS
See page 44.

BACK
With 2¾mm (No 12/US 2) needles, cast on 128 (134:142:148) sts. K 5 rows.
Change to 3¼mm (No 10/US 3) needles.
Inc row (right side): K19 (20:22:23), k twice in next st, [k21 (22:23:24), k twice in next st] 4 times, k20 (21:23:24). [133 (139:147:153) sts.]
Next row: K4, p to last 4 sts, k4.
Next row: K51 (54:58:61), sl 1, k29, sl 1, k to end.
Rep last 2 rows until Back measures 6 (7:7:8)cm/2¼ (2¾:2¾:3)in from beg, ending with a wrong side row.

Next row: K51 (54:58:61), sl 1, k29, sl 1 k to end.
Next row: P.
Rep last 2 rows until Back measures 30 (33:36:39)cm/11¾ (13:14¼:15¼)in from beg, ending with a wrong side row.
Shape Armholes
Cast off 6 (6:8:8) sts at beg of next 2 row Dec 1 st at each end of next 5 rows. [111 (117: 121: 127) sts.] Cont straight until armholes measure 8 (9:10:11)cm/3¼ (3¾:4:4½)in, ending with a wrong side row.
Next row: K41 (44:46:49), cast off next sts, k to end.
Next row: P40 (43:45:48), p2 tog, p to end. [81 (87:91:97) sts.]
Mark each end of last row. Work 3 rows i st st. Mark each end of last row. Cont in s st for a further 6cm/2¼in, ending with a p row.
Shape Neck
Next row: K29 (31:32:34), turn.
Work on this set of sts only. Dec 1 st at neck edge on next 4 rows. [25 (27:28:30) sts.] Cont straight until armholes measure 19 (20:21:22) cm/7½ (8:8¼:8¾) in, endi with a p row. Cast off.
With right side facing, slip centre 23 (25:27:29) sts on to a holder, rejoin yarn rem sts and k to end. Complete as given first side.

FRONT
With 2¾mm (No 12/US 2) needles, cast 99 (105:113:119) sts. K 5 rows.
Change to 3¼mm (No 10/US 3) needles.
Inc row: K19 (21:21:23), [k twice in ne st, k19 (20:22:23)] to end. [103 (109:117:123) sts.]

xt row: K4, p to last 4 sts, k4.
xt row: K.
o last 2 rows until Front measures 6
7:8)cm/2¼ (2¾:2¾:3)in from beg,
ling with a wrong side row. Beg with a k
v, work in st st across all sts until Front
asures 26 (29:32:35)cm/10¼ (11½:
¼:13¾)in from beg, ending with a p
.

ide for Opening
xt row: K48 (51:55:58), turn; leave rem
on a spare needle.
rk on first set of sts only.
xt row: Cast on 7 sts, k7, p to end.
(58:62:65) sts.]
xt row: K.
xt row: K7, p to end.
o last 2 rows until Front measures same
Back to armhole shaping, ending at side
e.

ape Armhole
st off 6 (6:8:8) sts at beg of next row.
rk 1 row. Dec 1 st at armhole edge on
t 5 rows. [44 (47:49:52) sts.] Cont
ight until armhole measures 11
:13:14)cm/4¼ (4¾:5:5½)in, ending at
hole edge.

ape Neck
xt row: Patt to last 12 (13:14:15) sts,
n; leave the 12 (13:14:15) sts on a safety

: 1 st at neck edge on every row until 25
:28:30) sts rem. Cont straight for a few
s until armhole measures 14
16:17)cm/5½ (6:6¼:6¾)in, ending with
row. Cast off.

rk front edge of left side of opening to
cate 3 buttons: first one 4 (5:3:4)cm/1½
¼:1½)in up from beg of opening, last
3 (3:4:4)cm/1¼ (1¼:1½:1½)in down
n neck edge and rem one evenly spaced
ween.
h right side facing, rejoin yarn to rem
k to end.
xt row: P to last 7 sts, k7.
xt row: K.
nplete as given for first side, making
onholes to match markers as follows:
tonhole row (right side): K2, k2 tog,
k to end.

LEFT SLEEVE
With 2¾mm (No 12/US 2) needles, cast on
52 (54:56:58) sts. K 5 rows.
Buttonhole row: K2, k2 tog, yf, k to end.
K 5 rows.
Change to 3¼mm (No 10/US 3) needles.
Next row: (K6 (6:7:7), k twice in next st) 5
times, k2 (4:0:2), turn. [42 (44:45:47) sts.]
Work on this set of sts only.
Next row: P to last 2 sts, k2.
Next row: K.
Rep last 2 rows 8 times more, then work
first of the 2 rows again, **at the same time**,
inc 1 st at beg of first row and 4 foll 4th
rows. [47 (49:50:52) sts.] Leave these sts
on a spare needle.
With right side facing, rejoin yarn at cuff to
rem 15 (15:16:16) sts, k to end.
Next row: K2, p to end.
Next row: K.
Rep last 2 rows 8 times more, inc 1 st at
end of first row and 3 foll 4th rows.
Next row: Cast off 2, p to last st, inc in last
st. [18 (18:19:19) sts.]
Next row: K to end, then k across sts on
spare needle. [65 (67:69:71) sts.]
** Beg with a p row, cont in st st, inc 1 st at
each end of 4th row and every foll 5th row
until there are 85 (89:95:99) sts. Cont
straight until Sleeve measures 28
(31:34:37)cm/11 (12¼:13½:14½)in from
beg, ending with a p row. Mark each end of
last row. Work a further 8 (8:10:10) rows.
Shape Top
Dec 1 st at each end of next 4 rows. Cast
off rem 77 (81:87:91) sts.

RIGHT SLEEVE
With 2¾mm (No 12/US 2) needles, cast on
52 (54:56:58) sts. K 5 rows.
Buttonhole row: K to last 4 sts, yf, k2 tog
tbl, k2.
K 5 rows.
Next row: K15 (15:16:16), turn.
Work on this set of sts only.
Next row: P to last 2 sts, k2.
Next row: K.
Rep last 2 rows 8 times more, **at the same
time**, inc 1 st at beg of first row and 3 foll
4th rows.

Next row: Inc in first st, p to last 2 sts, cast
off these 2 sts. [18 (18:19:19) sts.]
Leave these sts on a spare needle.
With right side facing, rejoin yarn at cuff to
rem 37 (39:40:42) sts.
Next row: K2 (4:0:2), [k twice in next st,
k6 (6:7:7)] 5 times. [42 (44:45:47) sts.]
Next row: K2, p to end.
Next row: K.
Rep last 2 rows 8 times more, then work
first of the 2 rows again, inc 1 st at end of
first row and 4 foll 4th rows. [47 (49:50:52)
sts.]
Next row: K to end, then k across sts on a
spare needle. [65 (67:69:71) sts.]
Complete as given for Left Sleeve from **.

NECKBAND
Join shoulder seams.
With right side facing and using 2¾mm
(No 12/US 2) needles, sl sts from right
front neck safety pin on to needle, pick up
and k12 sts up right front neck, 10 sts down
right back neck, k centre back sts while dec
3 sts evenly, pick up and k10 sts up left
back neck, 12 sts down left front neck, then
k2 tog, k10 (11:12:13) sts from left front
neck safety pin. [87 (91:95:99) sts.]
Next row: K to last 12 (13:14:15) sts, k2
tog, k to end.
K 2 rows. Work buttonhole row as given
for Front. K 4 rows. Cast off.

TO MAKE UP
Form pleat at centre of back and catch
down cast off sts on wrong side. Stitch
together top loops of sts on marked rows
on wrong side of back to form ridge on
right side. Sew on sleeves, sewing rows
above markers to cast off sts at armholes.
Beginning at top of borders, join side and
sleeve seams. Catch down button band on
wrong side at base of front opening. Catch
down the 2 cast off sts of sleeve opening
border on wrong side. Sew on buttons.
With crochet hook, make a buttonhole loop
on left side of pleat fold at waist position on
back. Sew button to other side.

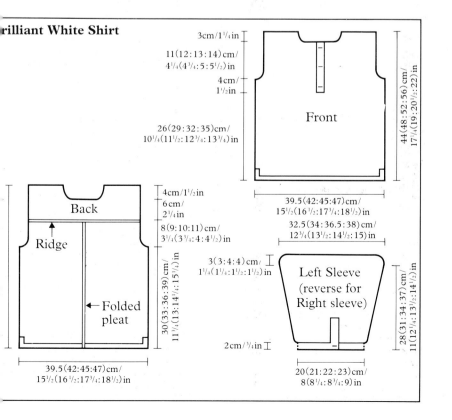

rilliant White Shirt

AUTHOR'S ACKNOWLEDGEMENTS

I would like to thank the following people for their invaluable help: Pat Church, Tina Egleton, Penny Hill, Maisie Lawrence and Frances Wallace.

I am particularly grateful to Tina Egleton for the pattern-checking, Sandra Lousada for the beautiful photography and Marie Willey for the perfect styling. I would also like to thank Will Brown for his patient assistance. Heather Jeeves, my agent, has as always provided unfailing support.

I would also like to thank the following children, and their mums, dads and carers: Beau, Corby, Hannah, Harley, Isabella, Jamie, Jasmine, Jeanne, Josie, Katie, Mica, Mickey and Nell.

The props and locations were provided by Old Town, Norwich.

ROWAN YARNS ADDRESSES

Rowan yarns can be obtained from stockists of good-quality knitting yarns. In case of difficulty in obtaining yarns, write to the addresses below for a list of stockists in your area.

U.K.: Rowan Yarns, Green Lane Mill, Holmfirth, West Yorkshire, England HD7 1RW
Tel: (01484) 681881

U.S.A.: Westminster Trading Corporation, 5 Northern Boulevard, Amherst, NH 03031
Tel: (603) 886 5041/5043

Australia: Rowan (Australia), 191 Canterbury Road, Canterbury, Victoria 3126
Tel: (03) 830 1609

Belgium: Hedera, Pleinstraat 68, 3001 Leuven
Tel: (016) 23 21 89

Canada: Estelle Designs & Sales Ltd, Units 65/67, 2220 Midland Avenue, Scarborough, Ontario M1P 3E6
Tel: (416) 298 9922

Denmark: Designer Garn, Vesterbro 33A, DK-9000 Aalborg
Tel: 98 13 48 24

France: Elle Tricote, 52 Rue Principale, 67300 Schiltigheim
Tel: (33) 88 62 6531

Germany: Wolle & Design, Wolfshovener Strasse 76, 52428 Julich Stetternich
Tel: (49) 2461 54735

Holland: Henk & Henrietta Beukers, Dorpsstraat 9, NL 5327 AR Hurwenen
Tel: 04182 1764

Iceland: Stockurinn, Kjorgardi, Laugavegi 59, ICE-101 Reykjavik
Tel: (01) 18254

Italy: La Compagnia del Cotone, Vi Mazzini 44, I-10123 Torino
Tel: (011) 87 83 81

Japan: Diakeito Co Ltd, 2-3-11 Senb Higashi, Minoh City, Osaka 562
Tel: 0727 27 6604

New Zealand: John Q Goldingham L PO Box 45083, Epuni Railway, Low Hutt
Tel: (04) 5674 085

Norway: Eureka, PO Box 357, N-14 Ski
Tel: 64 86 55 40

Sweden: Wincent, Sveavagen 94, 11 50 Stockholm
Tel: (08) 673 70 60